Geek's Gu: Wizarding ···· ·· Harry Potter

at Universal Orlando

An Unofficial Guide for Muggles and Wizards

Mary deSilva

Recent books by Mary deSilva

KIDS RULE! At Universal Orlando 2024

Copycat Recipes for the Wizarding World of Harry Potter at Universal Orlando

Geek's Guide to the Wizarding World of Harry Potter at Universal Orlando 2023

Universal Orlando Magic Tips 2023

Fantastic Eats and Where to Find Them at Universal Orlando 2022

#DrinkingUniversal 2022

Fantastic Drinks and Where to Find Them at Universal Orlando 2021

Cruise Tips: My Big Fat Greek Cruise Vacation

DEDICATION

For Emily

CONTENTS

A portion of the proceed from sales of this book benefit brain cancer research and Kelly Kicking Cancer, a 100% volunteer organization dedicated to eradicating brain cancer through fundraising. For more information, please visit:

www.KellyKickingCancer.org
#KellyKickingCancer

ACKNOWLEDGMENTS

My heartfelt thanks go out to several people for their help and encouragement in writing this, the sixth edition of this book. Thanks to Barbara Twardowski, my travel writing mentor and dear friend. Barbara, you are best travel writer I know. Thanks to Susan O'Mahoney for traveling with me to Orlando several times a year, listening to my ideas, offering unbiased critiques and editing.

Thanks to Trevor Aydelotte for his gorgeous cover photo of the dragon atop Gringotts.

Special thanks Kelly C. O'Mahoney. Her courage while battling brain cancer, gave me the courage to bring my travel writing ideas to reality.

Lastly and most importantly, I thank my family. Thanks to Jim for the many trips to Florida which have inspired my ideas for more writing and for putting up with me while I got that last idea down. Thank you Patrick for encouraging me to read all of the Harry Potter books which set me on a path to becoming a Harry Potter geek! Thanks to Emily for being my Orlando buddy. Your astute observations often astound me and your Harry Potter Geek enthusiasm inspire.

LETTER TO THE WIZARDING AND MUGGLE COMMUNITY

To Whom it May Concern:

Allow me to introduce myself. I am Nigel Wrightwood. I hold the office of Muggle Relations Ambassador for the Ministry of Magic. I serve this post by filling in for Marianna Blackwater while she is on a thrilling assignment in Arizona (I'm told on a matter involving Thunderbirds). My chief purpose today is to serve as an ambassador to muggles touring the Wizarding World of Harry Potter at Universal Orlando. This muggle resort is located in the state of Florida, within the enchanted city of Orlando, the home of many wizards and witches who began bewitching muggles with magical experiences since the year, 1971.

To recap the procession of—shall we say "Muggles to Magic," many years ago, a clever wizard called Walter Disney created his muggle resort in Orlando but kept magic a thinly veiled secret. In 1971, he had the audacity to create a "Magic Kingdom" which featured magical attractions and fantastic beasts (talking bears, flying elephants, etc). It is rumored that he had assistance to build his "kingdom" by a rather popular witch, Mary Poppins, who performed with no respect for magical secrecy. The park opened to fascinated muggles who willingly spent their currency. After Disney passed away, the secret was kept by the wizards who followed, and his kingdom was expanded upon to attract muggles from the world over. The creation of the *Magic Kingdom* upset many in the magical community who felt that his "world" was in direct violation of the 1692 International Statute of Secrecy, which made it unlawful for magic to be performed in the presence of muggles. This was blatant misuse. After all, who would dispute the fact that Walt Disney's house elf, Mickey, was the inspiration for his most famous character, a talking mouse!

Years later in Great Britain, a clever witch called J. K. Rowling also broke the secrecy statute by writing a series of books chronicling the life of a young wizard, Harry Potter, who became famous as"The boy who lived," and for the defeat of "He Who Must Not Be Named," the greatest dark wizard of all time. Her series of books were made into films which in turn made Ms. Rowling a very rich witch. She became very famous among muggles (although many in the wizarding community speculate that she used the Confundus Curse on the Minister for Magic for allowing this blatant violation of the secrecy statute). These books gave muggles an unprecedented glimpse into the world of magic.

The books and subsequent films so enraptured such a great number of muggles around the world, that they lead to a peculiar event in history. In 2010, the current Minister for Magic, Tarquin Littlefair, in an unprecedented move, gave a special waiver of the International Statute of Secrecy, and subsequently allowed the top wizards at Universal Orlando to duplicate the Village of Hogsmeade and Hogwarts Castle. While the reasons for this move are highly debated, there is no question that the Universal Orlando wizards, using magic, created an uncanny version of Hogsmeade. The result of the opening of the new Hogsmeade was that muggles from all over the world flocked to the land of Orlando to see Hogwarts Castle, buy chocolate frogs, wands, wizard gear.

In 2014, the savvy wizards at Universal Orlando once again petitioned the Minister For Magic to extend the waiver to recreate Diagon Alley. In another unprecedented move, magical wands (which muggles call Interactive Wands) were offered for sale at Ollivanders and other shops. What a controversy! Now muggles can practice casting spells at many locations throughout Diagon Alley and Hogsmeade! When the wizards of Slytherin House were particularly outraged, they were offered a compromise to the original plan and it was amended to include the addition of

Knockturn Alley, an area focused on the dark arts.

On a side note, Arthur Weasley was an invaluable consultant with his vast knowledge of muggle artifacts. This knowledge was especially valuable when he was consulted on the creation of enchanted motorbikes for a ride honoring Rubeus Hagrid. After all, it was Mr. Weasley who originally helped his close friend, Sirius Black, build the one of which the ride was inspired.

Magically Yours,

Nigel Wrightwood
Muggle Relations Ambassador
Ministry of Magic, London

INTRODUCTION

Welcome muggles, witches and wizards to the Wizarding World of Harry Potter at Universal Orlando! Included in this informative volume is a wealth of information to assist muggles in navigating through one of the world's most popular destinations, the magical land of Orlando, Florida. Witches and wizards as well as muggles are welcomed to visit Universal Orlando, the true home of sanctioned "magic." J. K. Rowling's stories about "the boy who lived" provide a perfect setting for muggles to experience and make a little magic and enchantments. These stories have brought such delight to muggles, that many have taken to describing themselves as "Potter Geeks." This "geek's guide" is dedicated to helping these muggles to explore, taste, smell and even cast spells!

In the following chapters, we will follow Harry Potter's steps through his world of magic—but beware! There are many spoilers in this book for first time visitors of the Wizarding World of Harry Potter! Throughout this volume, I have provided *Winks*—magical hints—sometimes referred to as Easter eggs, to enhance your experience and help you discover those hidden gems placed for muggle enjoyment and wizarding mirth. Also included throughout this volume are 30 Wizard Trivia Questions to test if you are a true "Harry Potter Geek!"

Tip: Download the digital ebook version of this book to your smart phone. In doing so, you will have expert magical advice at your fingertips!

Note: At the time of publication, the information in this book was accurate. However, all information provided is subject to change at any time.

Wink: *It is no secret in the wizarding world that Yen Sid, the sorcerer in the famous Disney film,* **Fantasia***, who sports a very tall hat, bears a striking resemblance to Albus Dumbledore.*

"We are only as strong as we are united, as weak as we are divided."
Albus Dumbledore
Harry Potter and the Goblet of Fire

CHAPTER 1: BUYING TICKETS FOR THE WIZARDING WORLD

The clever wizards at Universal Orlando, in an attempt to ban any misuse of muggle entertainment, have cast many charms and enchantments on the Wizarding World of Harry Potter. Both muggles, as well as wizards and witches, traveling to Orlando must purchase admission tickets to Universal Orlando to access entry into Hogsmeade and Diagon Alley.

Tickets for Admission to the Wizarding World

Muggles and magical folk may purchase tickets at the entrance gates of Universal Orlando Resort. A more effective way, however, is to visit the muggle website, www.UniversalOrlando.com. By using this website, muggles may save about $20 American dollars on their tickets. If are staying multiple days, there are several ticket options to consider. The Harry Potter sections of the theme parks, Diagon Alley and Hogsmeade, can be extremely busy and crowded no matter what time of year you visit adding extra days to your visit is highly recommended. No matter how many days you want to spend, be sure to choose the Park-to-Park option. This is the only way that you may travel between Hogsmeade and Diagon Alley on the Hogwarts Express train.

The current prices and ticket options are as follows (but subject to change by the crafty Universal Orlando wizards at any time):

Warning: Don't purchase tickets from unknown vendors or online sites like Craigslist.com. While the passes might be valid, many travelers have been burned by purchasing these passes. Many travelers have arrived at the gates and been denied entrance due to invalid passes. Buy tickets online, through a wholesale club, like Samsclub.com, use a travel agent or a safe discount site with a good reputation like www.UndercoverTourist.com. This site also has a useful crowd calendar.

FYI: All tickets and annual passes are non-transferable.

Types of Tickets

Tickets are available as One-Day tickets, Multiple-Day Tickets or Annual Passes and for an extra fee may include entrance to a water park. When purchasing online, you may choose one of these options:

One Park Per Day tickets include access to either Universal Studios or Islands of Adventure for one day during park hours. This type of ticket excludes the Hogwarts Express train ride.

Park to Park tickets (similar to Disney's Park Hopper) allows unlimited access to two or three parks for one day during park hours. This type of ticket is required to ride the Hogwarts Express train ride in The Wizarding World of Harry Potter.

- Two-Park Tickets include the two main theme parks— Universal Studios and Islands of Adventure.

- Three-Park Tickets include the addition of Volcano Bay Waterpark.

Ticket Combinations

Combo tickets are available in two types. With multi-day tickets, you may choose between Two-Park Ticket Combos and Three-Park Ticket Combos. Two park ticket options are listed below. Ticket combos are also available with the Park to Park option and the One Park Per Day option.

Note: An Adult is age 10 years and up. Child tickets are for children ages 3-9 years. Children up to age 2 years get in free. Prices shown are per person and do not include tax or shipping.

Note: Prices change according to the date selected. The prices listed are the lowest prices available but depending on your date of travel, they may be significantly higher. These prices are subject to change.

Park to Park Tickets

This type of ticket is available for one day or multiple days. The more days you buy, the more you save. **Park to Park access is required to ride the Hogwarts Express train ride which travels between the two main parks.**

2-Park—Park to Park Tickets

	Adult	Child
1 Day Ticket	From $174	From $169
2 Day Tickets	From $293	From $283
3 Day Tickets	From $315.99	From $306
4 Day Tickets	From $337	From $327
5 Day Tickets	From $360	From $350

2-Park, One Park Per Day Tickets

	Adult	Child
1 Day Ticket	From $119	From $114
2 Day Ticket	From $233	From $223
3 Day Ticket	From $255.99	From $246
4 Day Ticket	From $272	From $262
5 Day Ticket	From $290	From $280

Volcano Bay Water Theme Park Tickets

	Adult	Child
1 Day Ticket	80.00	75.00

Three park ticket combos are available at an increased rate. These ticket combos include Universal Studios, Islands of Adventure and Volcano Bay Water Theme Park.

Wink: *If you visit more than once a year, the best value is an annual pass. See the section below.*

Ticket Delivery Options

There are two options to receive your tickets:

Mobile Ticket. Delivery by e-mail and can be added to the "wallet" on the Universal app or smartphone's Wallet.

*Will Call. Will Call Kiosk's are located near the entrance to each theme park but also at Onsite Resorts in the lobby near the Concierge desk. You may also pick up tickets at ticket window and Guest Services locations in CityWalk and outside the entrance of each park. Will Call Kiosks dispense credit card sized paper card tickets.

Geek Tip: *Do not choose "Print Ticket" if offered. Printed paper tickets may get wet and be destroyed. The best option is Will Call.*

Call Guest Services for more information at (407) 224-4233.

Annual Passes

If you will be visiting Universal Orlando for three days or more, instead of buying Park to Park tickets, you may want to purchase an annual pass. The Seasonal pass is close to the same price as a 4-day Park-to-Park pass, although there are black out dates. Each of these entitles the passholder to 365 days beginning at the first use! This means you can purchase your tickets now before the prices go up! Annual Passholders also get up to a 30% discount when they renew!

FlexPay is also available as a monthly payment plan with automatic renewal. However, you will pay more in the end when using FlexPay. For more information, visit universalorlando.com.

FYI: Florida residents get a discount!

There are four types of annual passes, listed in order of lowest price to highest:

Seasonal Annual Pass
Annual Power Pass
Annual Preferred Pass
Annual Premier Pass

All annual passes include benefits such as unlimited Park-to-Park access, onsite hotel discounts, special event discounts and special vacation packages.

All annual passes include these great benefits:

• Includes admission to select special events such as Mardi Gras and Holidays (concerts not included)
• Special discounts on separately ticketed events such as Halloween Horror Nights

- 10% off Multi-Day theme park tickets purchased at the front gate (up to six tickets per transaction; not valid on 3-Park Unlimited tickets, Universal Express passes or tickets with Universal Express)
- Save up to 30% off base rates plus enjoy a free single car class upgrade at Budget® and Avis®
- Admission to the Passholder Lounge presented by Coca-Cola® inside Universal Studios Florida
- $1 off per Coca-Cola Freestyle® additional day recharge
- Passholder Game Play Pass - $25 for 6 game plays (one additional play for free)
- $3 off admission to after 6pm showings at Universal Cinemark for Passholder and up to one guest (excludes Senior Mondays, $5 Tuesdays and matinées).

Note: Free parking with purchase of two Universal Cinemark matinée tickets

Onsite Hotel Annual Pass Benefits:

Hard Rock Hotel®:
- 10% off food and non-alcoholic beverages at The Kitchen.
- 10% off food and non-alcoholic beverages at Velvet Lounge (not valid for special events and holidays)

Loews Royal Pacific Resort:
- 10% off food and non-alcoholic beverages at Islands Dining Room
- 10% off food and non-alcoholic beverages at Orchid Court Lounge & Sushi Bar (not valid for special events and holidays)

Loews Sapphire Falls Resort:
- 10% off food and non-alcoholic beverages at Amatista Cookhouse
- 10% off food and non-alcoholic beverages at Strong Water Tavern (not valid for special events and holidays)

Universal's Cabana Bay Beach Resort:
- 10% off food and non-alcoholic beverages at all dining outlets
- 10% off tubes at the Tube Shack
- 10% off cabana rentals
- 15% off food and non-alcoholic beverages at Galaxy Bowl with the purchase of bowling
- 10% off Sonic souvenir cups

Universal's Aventura Hotel:
- 10% off all food and non-alcoholic beverages at all dining outlets (not valid for special events and holidays)
- 10% off Sonic souvenir cups (not valid for special events and holidays)

Universal's Endless Summer Resort – Surfside Inn & Suites:
- 10% off all food and non-alcoholic beverages at all dining outlets (not valid for special events and holidays)
- 10% off Sonic Souvenir Cup (not valid for special events and holidays)

Universal's Endless Summer Resort – Dockside Inn & Suites:
- 10% off all food and non-alcoholic beverages at all dining outlets (not valid for special events and holidays)
- 10% off Sonic Souvenir Cup (not valid for special events and holidays)

Annual Pass Prices and Benefits

	Seasonal	Power	Preferred	Premier
2 Park, US and IOA	$424.99	$474.99	$629.99	$904.99
3 Park, US, IOA, VB	$524.99	$584.99	$739.99	1,094.9
Park to Park Access	yes	yes	yes	Yes

8

	Seasonal	Power	Preferred	Premier
Universal Express after 4pm	No	No	No	Yes
Free self parking	No	Discounted	yes	yes
Free Valet parking	No	No	No	No
Early Park Admission	No	No	block out dates	yes
Dining and Shopping Discounts	No	No	yes	yes
Onsite Hotel Discounts	yes	yes	yes	yes
Special events & concerts	No	yes	yes	yes
One free HHN ticket	No	No	No	yes

Block Out Dates

Power Annual Pass

Blockout Dates for Universal's Islands of Adventure and Universal Studios Florida:

December 23 – 31, 2023
January 1 – 2, 2024
March 18 – March 30, 2024
December 21 - 31, 2024
January 1 – 5, 2025
April 7 – April 19, 2025

Blockout Dates for Universal's Volcano Bay:
June 10 – August 13, 2023, Blockouts apply before 4 pm
June 8 – August 11, 2024, Blockouts apply before 4 pm

Power Passholders are blocked out of Universal Studios Florida only until 5pm on concert dates if there is a concert on a blockout date. Concert dates will be announced at a later date and are subject to change.

Seasonal Annual Pass

Blockout Dates for Universal's Islands of Adventure and Universal Studios Florida:
July 1 – July 31, 2023
December 23 – 31, 2023
January 1 – 2, 2024
March 18 – April 6, 2024
July 1 – 31, 2024
November 25 - 30, 2024
December 21 - 31, 2024
January 1 – 5, 2025
April 7 – April 26, 2025

Seasonal Passholders are blocked out of Universal Studios Florida on all concert dates. Concert dates will be announced at a later date and are subject to change.

Blockout Dates for Universal's Volcano Bay:
April 1 – April 8, 2023
June 10 – August 13, 2023
March 18 – April 6, 2024
June 8 – August 11, 2024
April 7 - April 26, 2025

"It is our choices, Harry, that show what we truly are, far more than our abilities."
Albus Dumbledore
Harry Potter and the Chamber of Secrets

CHAPTER 2: UNIVERSAL'S ONSITE RESORTS

The Universal Orlando wizards have divulged many wizarding secrets, but letting muggles spend nights in the wizarding world is going a bit too far. The Minister For Magic has decreed that some secrets must be kept from muggles. There are no available guest rooms in either The Leaky Cauldron or in the Village of Hogsmeade for muggles at Universal Orlando. So where can muggles and wizards rest their weary heads?

Onsite Resorts

Touring the Wizarding World of Harry Potter is exhilarating but also quite an exhausting experience, even for wizards and witches. After a long day, what could be better than to relax at a luxury resort right on the property?

Magical and non-magical guests have their choice when it comes to lodging in Orlando. There are locals inns ranging far and wide. However, if you are going to spend the majority of your time at the Wizarding World of Harry Potter, the best choice is a Universal Orlando onsite resort. There are eight onsite hotels from which to choose and each has its own unique theme and amenities. All onsite resorts are run by the Loews family of hotels, which is quite an enterprising group of muggles who are known for their dedication to quality lodging.

Tip: Guests at each onsite resort can enjoy free transportation to the parks, Early Park Admission, and package delivery to the resort for purchases made in the parks.

There are several categories for onsite resorts which are listed below.

Premier Resorts

The three original onsite resorts offer the finest accommodations at Universal Orlando and also offer special benefits to their guests, the greatest value of which is complimentary **Universal Express**. Although these resorts offer the same benefits, they are managed independently from Universal and each premier resort has its own distinct "personality." Each of these resorts is within walking distance and water taxis are also available.

Loews Portofino Bay Resort

In what seems a feat of magic, the Loews team of muggles have recreated the Italian Riviera in Orlando at Loews Portofino Bay Resort. This Italian inspired "seaside" resort is the most luxurious and well equipped resort at

Universal Orlando. The overall Italian theme is present everywhere at this resort, from the grapevines as you enter the drive to the decor and the amazing dining choices. The resorts has 750 guest rooms, 45 suites, 7 restaurants, a spa, a concierge floor, fitness room, and three swimming pools. The hotel offers something special for little ones and families—the **Despicable Me Kids Suites**, two bedroom suites with a Minion theme in a separate children's bedroom.

Hard Rock Hotel

American Muggles love their rock 'n roll music stars and at the Hard Rock Hotel, each guest is treated like a VIP rock star. The property has 650 guest rooms, including 29 suites including Future Rock Star Kids Suites, and a 12,000 square foot guitar shaped pool, and other entertainments such as a water slide, sandpit for children and another feat of muggle ingenuity—under-water speakers playing rock music. The resort has a pool bar and grill as well as hotel bar and restaurants, both casual and fine dining. The Hard Rock Hotel is the nearest onsite hotel to the entrance to Universal Studios—only a short five minute walk.

Loews Royal Pacific Resort

Whether or not you have visited the south seas, you will recognize the lush landscape, exotic palms, sandy beaches and peaceful tranquility at the Loews Royal Pacific Resort. The property has 1,000 guest rooms, 51 suites and Jurassic Park Kids Suites. The hotel has a lagoon style pool with a water slide. Conde Nast Traveler gave this resort their Readers' Choice Award in the "Top 150 Resorts in Mainland U.S." for two years in a row. The resort also received the top slot in Travel + Leisure Magazine's "Top 50—Best Family Resorts in the U. S. and Canada" list more than once. There are several dining options from which to choose including a grand sushi bar and lounge, an American grill, a family restaurant, coffee shop and a luau dinner show. Guests at this resort may experience a tranquility found no where else at Universal Orlando.

Premier Resort Benefits:

- Free Universal Express — Unlimited ride access to skip the regular lines in both theme parks (not available on the two most popular Harry Potter rides).
- Early park admission to the Wizarding World of Harry Potter one hour before the theme park opens (valid theme park admission required).
- Complimentary water taxis and shuttle buses to both theme parks and CityWalk.
- Priority seating and discounts at select restaurants throughout both theme parks and CityWalk.
- Access to pool areas at all onsite resorts.
- Merchandise purchased at the parks or CityWalk may delivered to your room.
- Free WiFi
- Keurig Coffee Makers

In addition to these benefits, each premier hotel offers **Club Level** (concierge) rooms with these additional benefits:

- Evening turndown service, and cotton signature bathrobes
- Access to a private lounge
- Personal concierge services to help with all your vacation needs
- Complimentary coffee, assorted teas, and soft drinks throughout the day
- Continental breakfast served each morning
- Hot & cold hors d'oeuvres and entrees as well as complimentary beer and wine
- Dessert treats each night

Preferred Resort

Loews Sapphire Falls Resort

The Caribbean themed Loews Sapphire Falls Resort is a moderately priced resort with the feel of a luxury resort. It is located between Royal Pacific Resort and Cabana Bay Beach Resort. The atmosphere transports guests to a Caribbean paradise where blue waterfalls cascade into sparkling pools. The resort is a tropical jewel with a luxuriously landscaped 16,000 square foot pool surrounded by waterfalls. "Ruins" of a stone turret are the centerpiece of the modern-chic lobby. The 1,000 guest rooms and suites are designed with a focus on comfort. The resort's design is based on old-world of the Caribbean while still being chic and modern.

Dining options include a full-service restaurant with a view of the water, a poolside bar and grill, a great "rum bar" and grill with knowledgeable "Rum Captains," and a quick service coffee shop offering ice cream, grab & go meals and Caribbean-style hot entrees. The hotel also offers a fitness center with a dry sauna, the largest resort pool, a water slide, fire pits, a children's play area, and cabana rentals.

Prime Value Resorts

Universal's Cabana Bay Beach Resort

Guests traveling with families will appreciate the amenities and value offered at Universal's Cabana Bay Beach Resort. It features a fun retro theme that takes you back to the iconic beach resorts of the 1950's and 60's. Just because it is less expensive, doesn't mean that there aren't numerous incredible amenities to enjoy. Guests staying here enjoy two giant swimming pools with a waterslide, lazy river, 10-lane bowling alley, and an exclusive entrance to Volcano Bay Water Park. The hotel features very popular family suites as well as regular hotel rooms and two-bedroom suites. The hotel is within walking distance of the theme parks and

Universal CityWalk's dining and entertainment complex. Guests have use the complimentary shuttle buses. The resort's dining options include a food court serving breakfast, lunch and dinner, Starbucks, Galaxy Bowl Restaurant, poolside grills and a lobby bar.

Universal's Aventura Hotel

The Aventura Hotel is a very modern glass high rise structure with a modern-retro styled lobby. Each of the guest rooms has is equipped with a tablet which controls the lights and television (wizards have a bit of trouble with these muggle features). There is an open air rooftop restaurant and bar with fantastic food and the hotel has other dining options including Starbucks and a great food court—try the gelato!

Wink: *The Aventura Hotel is shaped like the muggle fad toy, a fidget spinner!*

Value Resorts

Universal's Endless Summer Resort

Because not all wizards and muggles are as rich as the Malfoy's, more economical hotel options are available onsite. It is truly magical, the amount of amenities provided at such a low price at these Endless Summer Resort sister hotels. They are located "off-site, but are still on-site" resorts. These two hotels are the only onsite resorts which are not walking distance to the theme parks. Complimentary shuttle bus transportation to the theme parks is included as well as Early Park Admission to enter the Wizarding World of Harry Potter one hour prior to the stated opening time. These two resorts offer the greatest value with weekday rates as low as $99!

Surfside Inn and Suites opened in 2019 and is located on Universal Boulevard—only a 5 minute drive to the theme parks. The resort includes 750 guest rooms including 390 2-Bedroom Suites which sleep six. The 2-Bedroom suites are the best deal for families with 3 queen size beds, a kitchenette with microwave, refrigerator, and single cup coffee maker (no coffee maker in standard rooms). Like all onsite resorts, there is complimentary transportation to the theme parks, CityWalk and Volcano Bay Waterpark. For recreation, there is a large surfboard-shaped pool and splash pad as well as a large complimentary fitness center and game room with high end arcade games.

Surfside Inn's sister hotel, **Dockside Inn and Suites**, is the newest onsite resort which opened in December of 2020. It is across the street from its sister hotel on Universal Boulevard and the rooms are practically identical to Surfside's. Dockside has two large pool areas with pool bars offering snacks and lots of lounge chair seating. Other dining options include a large food court and Starbucks. Accommodations include the very popular two bedroom suites as well as basic hotel rooms with two queen beds (only suites have in room coffee makers).

"Anyone can speak Troll. All you have to do is point and grunt."
Fred Weasley
Harry Potter and the Goblet of Fire

ABOUT | ATTRACTIONS & MORE

UNIVERSAL STUDIOS FLORIDA

The Wizarding World of Harry Potter™ - Diagon Alley™

LAND OVERVIEW

Follow in Harry Potter's footsteps as you walk through the streets of London, and enter Diagon Alley™ where you'll find many of the wizarding world's most famous establishments. Dine at the Leaky Cauldron™, see a wand choose a wizard at Ollivanders™ wand shop, and get ready to travel deep below Gringotts™ bank for a multi-dimensional thrill ride.

 Home Map Buy Profile

CHAPTER 3: A MAGICAL APP FOR A MAGICAL JOURNEY

For muggles with smartphones, downloading the Universal Orlando app can be an essential part of a successful experience at the Wizarding World of Harry Potter. Although it is not essentially required, unlike at Disney World, there are a some very important features on the app for muggles, especially when the parks are at their busiest.

Upon opening the app, on the Home screen under "Things to Do," there are two tabs of interest to muggles. One of these tabs with Harry's picture is for Diagon Alley and one is for Hogsmeade. Tap each of these tabs and tap "Attractions and More" right under Harry's picture. This will give you a list of attractions, shows, dining and shops in each park. It is a good idea to look through these when deciding which park to enter first—most muggles prefer to experience the magic just like Harry did by choosing Diagon Alley first!

Useful App Uses

The Universal Orlando has many features which can be very helpful on your magical journey through this land.

Uses For The App:

Buy Tickets
Storage of Mobile Tickets*
Set Up Universal Pay
Find Park Hours
Set a Parking Reminder
Find maps to attractions, dining and shopping
Mobile food and drink ordering
Virtual Ride Times

And much more!

*While mobile tickets are an efficient option, if the app experiences difficulties or problems with your phone's battery, you may not be able to access your tickets. My favorite option for acquiring tickets is "Will Call." Your tickets will be in the "Wallet" section of the app. If staying onsite, pick up your tickets at your hotel kiosk, concierge or pick up at any Guest Services location.

Mobile Food and Drink Ordering

A useful and at times essential feature on the app is Mobile Ordering. During times when the theme parks are very busy, most of the quick service restaurants, which include The Leaky Cauldron and The Three Broomsticks, enact Mobile Ordering. This feature allows guest to skip the lines and order food or drinks (non-alcoholic) from your smartphone. You can set your order in advance of arriving at the restaurant. Be sure to check out the side items, because there are often menu offerings you may prefer.

How to Order Food on the App?

- Open the Home tab on the app
- Tap "Order Food & Drinks"
- Select the restaurant—Restaurants are listed by area, starting with CityWalk
- Add menu items to your order, confirm and check out
- Premier and Preferred Annual Passholders, tap "Apply Passholder Discount" and scan your Pass bar code.
- When you arrive at the restaurant, tap "Prepare My Order."
- At the Leaky Cauldron or Three Broomsticks, check in with a Team Member to be seated and wait for your order to arrive.

Virtual Ride Times

Another useful feature is generally only enacted when the park is very busy—you will know when it is necessary when the Virtual Ride Times tab appears on the app's Home screen.

Virtual Ride Times became an essential reason for using the app when Hagrid opened his extremely popular motorbike ride. In the past when the last wizarding world ride opened, Harry Potter and the Escape from Gringotts, guests actually waited in line for six hours! The Universal Orlando managing muggles decided to enact Virtual Ride Times, to prevent such long wait times in queues. Now that these rides have been open a few years, the wait times have reduced to reasonable amounts of time, but can still rise on the most busy days. Therefore, use of this app feature can be essential if you want to experience Hagrid's motorbikes and all of his fantastic beasts!

How to Set a Virtual Ride Time:

1. If it is a busy time of year, arrive at the park on or before park opening time because there is a limited number of virtual times.
2. Before the theme park's official opening time, open the Universal Orlando app.
3. Open the Home tab and tap "Virtual Line Experience"
4. Tap the desired attraction
5. When the park opens, tap "Reserve" select the number of guests in your party, up to six and several virtual times should pop up.
6. Tap a time as fast as you can because they go quickly.
7. You will receive a code. Screenshot this code for just in case. There have been reports of guests being unable to access their code due to app problems.

Note: If you fail to get a time, ask the Team Member at the

ride entrance for assistance. Sometimes they offer virtual line times at different times during the day such as 9am, 11am and 2:00pm. If the team member is no help, visit a Guest Services location for assistance.

Wink: *Have other members of your party also try to get a virtual line time for more chances to ride!*

What is Unavailable on the App

There are a couple of features that Universal guests only wish they could do from the app. Unlike the Disney World app, there is no way to make dining reservations using the app. So what to do? This really is no issue in the wizarding world because only full service restaurants (table service with waiters) accept reservations. However, during your trip, you may feel the need to make a dining reservation. Mythos is a mystical themed restaurant right outside of Hogsmeade and is a favorite for guests. For more UK themed fare, Finnegan's Bar & Grill, an Irish pub, in the Universal Studios New York section is also a favorite.

Dining Reservations

Follow these instructions to make dining reservations at theme parks, onsite hotel restaurants and CityWalk restaurants.

How to Make a Dining Reservation on Your Phone

There are actually three ways to make a reservation, but I only recommend one way. You should make a reservation as far in advance as possible if you are travelings during a busy park time.

1. Call to make a reservation. For full service restaurants inside the theme parks, call (407) 224-3663.

2. Make reservations at the Full Service Restaurant touch screen at the entrance to each park. Ask a Team Member if you have trouble finding it. I don't recommend this option because it may be too late to get a reservation at your desired restaurant.

3. Make a reservation online by visiting UniversalOrlando.com. You may make a reservation from your smartphone by opening a the Universal online site on a web page. When you have the site open, tap the three horizontal lines on the top right, tap "Things to Do," tap "Dining" and scroll down to the restaurant and tap it.
4. Scroll down to Reservations and tap "online." Choose a date, number of guests, time and input your information.

Watch this video to learn how: https://www.youtube.com/watch?v=NonZFFG6Uoc&t=125s

Hotel Reservations

Another unavailable feature on the app is hotel reservations. Unlike the Disney app, you cannot make reservations on the app or get an Annual Passholder hotel discount. Not to worry, because directions to make reservations and get the discount are listed below.

How to Make a Hotel Reservation on Your Phone:

For Non-Passholders:

- Open the app and tap the three horizontal lines on the top right
- Scroll Down to "Places to Stay"
- Tap "Special Offers" for current offers or scroll to your desired hotel

- Scroll down and tap "Check Availability" and follow the prompts to make a reservation.

For Annual Passholders:

- Open the app and and tap the three horizontal lines on the top right
- Scroll all the way down and tap set tap on or off for Florida passholders
- Tap "Annual Passholders"
- Tap "Hotels and Packages"
- Scroll down and tap "Check Rates."

Note: These rates should include the passholder discount. If the hotel is near full capacity, a passholder rate may be unavailable.

Watch this video for more information:
https://www.youtube.com/watch?v=Ie6po67KL5Y&t=3s

"If you want to know what a man's like, take a good look at how he treats his inferiors, not his equals."
Sirius Black, *Harry Potter and the Goblet of Fire*

CHAPTER 4: THE LONDON WATERFRONT

U pon entering Universal Studios, muggles may experience a little confusion when looking for Diagon Alley. A stipulation to adhere to some degree of the Ministry of Magic's Secrecy Statute, there are no signs to direct muggles to the entrance of Diagon Alley. Accordingly, Universal has left no signage directing muggles to Diagon Alley. Many hapless muggles walk past the entrance—not realizing the wizardry of Diagon Alley taking place just beyond. However, at the London Waterfront, there are famous London landmarks and a very large hint that magic is near!

Photographic opportunities abound in this small gateway area between the San Francisco area and the World

Expo area. If you would like to experience magic just as Harry did, the London Waterfront should be your first stop on your way to Diagon Alley. Mind you, most muggles miss many details on their first trip. There are so many details to take in, so allow time in your schedule to peruse the area. The best advice is to arrive when the park opens—when many muggles are still in bed! If you have the time, slowly tour this area. Most muggles discover something new on each visit.

Warning: Spoilers! If you have never toured the Wizarding World of Harry Potter, the information found in this and the following chapter give many details. If you don't want any spoilers, read no further.

Diagon Alley Entrance and Charing Cross Road

Charing Cross Road is a short stretch of lane next to Kings Cross Station with shop fronts, a park and the Leaky Cauldron door with sign above. It is so unassuming, most muggles do not even notice this door. As written in the book, *Harry Potter and the Philosopher's Stone*, by J. K. Rowling:

> *"It was a tiny, grubby-looking pub. If Hagrid hadn't pointed it out, Harry would not have noticed it was there. The people hurrying by did not glance at it. Their eyes slid from the big book shop on one side to the record shop on the other as if they couldn't see the Leaky Cauldron at all."*

The door to this "inn" is located between Screed and Sons Book Shop and the Record Shop. No matter how many times you cast "Alohomora," the door will not open. The door looks as if it is part of Screed & Sons but the bricks above are darkened with age—a sign of old magic. Browse the shop windows on this stretch of lane for **Winks**. To the right of the door is the red bricked Leicester Station which is the nearest hidden entrance to Diagon Alley. There are also entrances to Diagon Alley at the famous London landmark, the Wyndham Theater. Across the lane is a park with the famous Eros Fountain from Piccadilly Circus.

Kings Cross Station

Flanking the left side of the London Waterfront area is Kings Cross Station. While it may seem to some to be just the queue for the Hogwarts Express, Kings Cross is much more. Musical performers called "street buskers" are very often stationed at the entrance . As you enter Kings Cross, relish the air conditioning which completes the London atmosphere—a feature which is delicious in the Florida heat. Take your time walking through the station and notice the themed advertisements on the walls. There is a large billboard advertisement which represents the Divine Magic billboard in front of which Dumbledore appeared to Harry Potter in the film, *Harry Potter and the Half Blood Prince*. While walking through the queue, between Platforms 9 and 10, there is a spot where you can "magically" walk through the bricks of Platform 9 3/4 before entering the wizarding train platform. This is an illusion of magic but it does allow muggles to take pictures of members of their party walking "through the brick wall."

Wink: *Upon entering Kings Cross Station, notice the train schedule board which is on London time and frequently changes.*

Wink: *Hermione's voice sounds distinctly different on the Hogwarts Express ride. It may be that this is Hermione's actual voice (not Emma Watson's, the actress) or just a mischievous charm by one of the*

Weasley brothers.

Wizard Trivia Question No. 1: Why did Harry Potter name his owl Hedwig?

The Red Telephone Booth

When you think of London, the most iconic image that comes to mind is the red telephone booth. The London Waterfront would not be complete without one. In the film, *Harry Potter and the Order of the Phoenix,* this telephone booth was the guest entry portal for wizards to enter the Ministry of Magic. The booth is located directly across from the Leaky Cauldron door and the entrance to Diagon Alley which many muggles fail to notice. The telephone booth is very popular with muggles for photos.

Wink: *Dial M-A-G-I-C (62442) on the phone in the red phone booth to connect to the Ministry of Magic.*

The Knight Bus

If you cannot find the entrance to Diagon Alley, there is a giant purple hint! Just look for the Knight Bus—it can't be missed! It is located next to the Eros Fountain. This purple triple decker bus is a mode of wizarding travel (other common modes include broomsticks, thestrals, apparition, and the Floo Network, all of which are banned from use at Universal Orlando) which takes travelers to all destinations —but nothing underwater.

One of the few Wizarding World character greetings is available at the Knight Bus. The conductor (with a great resemblance to Stan Shunpike) is there as well as the interactive talking shrunken head. Have a little chat with him and perhaps he will allow you peek inside the bus for photos.

Wink: This was the actual bus filmed in the movie, Harry Potter and the Prisoner of Azkaban.

Wizard Trivia Question No. 2: What name did Harry give the Knight Bus conductor when asked for his name in the book, *Harry Potter and the Prisoner of Azkaban*?

Wink: The Eros Fountain also called the Shaftesbury Memorial Fountain sits in Piccadilly Circus in London. The fountain is named for the 7th Earl of Shaftesbury who was famous for replacing child workhouses with schools. This would be a literary nod to the books of J. K. Rowling.

No. 12 Grimmauld Place

Grimmauld Place, a residential lane, is located in the London Borough of Islington. Number 12 Grimmauld Place is the ancestral home of the Black family, famous for dark magic. The house is represented at the London Waterfront in a row of brown brick homes. The bricks at number 12 are darkened because of all of the dark magic which has taken place inside.

Wink: Look up to the second floor window to occasionally see Kreacher, the Black family house elf, peeking out at all of the nosy Muggles.

London Taxi Huts

On either side of the London Waterfront, you will fine two green sheds which are London Taxi Huts. In London, these structures, sometimes referred to as "cab shelters," were originally the first "drive-through" food stops for hackney cab drivers. At the taxi hut across from Grimmauld Place, British street food is served with a menu of a variety of topped jacket potatoes (known as baked potatoes to American muggles), foot long hot dogs prepared to resemble sausage rolls, sodas, beer and crisps (chips) are sold here. Across from the record shop is another London Taxi Hut selling Knight Bus and Hogwarts Express merchandise.

Hogwarts Express—Kings Cross Station

The Hogwarts Express is the one and only "ride" in the London Waterfront. Like its namesake in the films, this unique train is one of a kind. It is the first of its kind in the muggle world—a "ride" from inside one theme park which brings riders into a different theme park. In Universal Studios Florida, the Hogwarts Express takes riders to Hogsmeade Station in Universal's Islands of Adventure, a completely different park. Park-to-Park admission tickets or annual passes are required to ride. The train compartments seat 8 passengers each in European style train compartment with air conditioning, cushioned seats and large "window" out of which from which riders encounter a few characters from the films. Notice the menacing Malfoy Manor on the way and try not to be frightened by Dementors! These chilling aspects are so brief, that all ages can ride easily and happily.

The Hogwarts Express is accessible and capable of carrying electronic conveyance vehicles (motorized scooters), wheelchairs and personal strollers. The Hogwarts Prefects will assist you to put your vehicle on the train for you and have it waiting for you in Hogsmeade.

"It takes a great deal of bravery to stand up to our enemies, but just as much to stand up to our friends."
Albus Dumbledore
Harry Potter and the Sorcerer's Stone

CHAPTER 5: DIAGON ALLEY

W onder abounds as you step through the opening in the bricks and take in your first sight of Diagon Alley! This is a very emotional moment for many muggles! In this unique area, magic is practiced daily by not only wizards but also by muggles!. Muggles have the unique opportunity to cast spells with exclusive interactive wands. If they desire, they may exchange U. S. muggle currency for Gringotts bank notes at Gringotts Money Exchange to use for purchases in the Wizarding World and and get a taste of wizards' brews available nowhere else in the world.

Plan to spend a significant part of your day in Diagon Alley because there is so much to see and experience. The magic is so immersive that after numerous visits, guests are still finding there is more magic to discover.

Diagon Alley is actually comprised of four "streets." Of course, there is Diagon Alley which is accessed at the Leicester Station entrance from the London Waterfront and the most popular way to enter the area. At the end of the lane, turn right onto Horizont Alley and proceed to Carkitt Market which leads back to Diagon Alley. The entrance to Knockturn Alley is just past entrance to the Leaky Cauldron on Diagon Alley.

Wink: *With the exception of the offshoot, Knockturn Alley, the Diagon Alley streets "diagonally" intersect to form a triangle.*

How to Find Diagon Alley

The clever Universal Studios wizards have done such a good job of disguising the entrance, that many a muggle walks past without any idea of the magic just beyond. They have however left a great clue in the form of the Knight Bus across from the entrance! Follow these directions to find Diagon Alley:

1. Enter Universal Studios through the giant arch and proceed through the turnstiles where park passes are

scanned. Proceed straight ahead through Minion Land to the New York Area.

2. Turn right at the Macy's store front and head straight through San Francisco until reaching The London Waterfront, where you will see the Knight Bus. Kings Cross Station will be in sight on the left.

3. Walk past the book shop and record shop and enter through the opening at Leicester Station.

4. Follow the path to the brick opening and take a moment to savor your first glimpse of the immersive wizarding world. The Leaky Cauldron is on the left (marked by the cracked cauldron sign). Many muggles have been reduced to tears at first sight of Diagon Alley!

Wink: *Examine the interesting "fountain" in the brick wall at the entrance (turn around when you see the opening in the bricks). It depicts a goblin statue crafted into a fountain with a fish spout. Perhaps this goblin was disgraced or a rival of the goblin, Gringott.*

Touring the Alley Street by Street

The streets or lanes of Diagon Alley are laid out in a "triangle" with the exception of Knockturn Alley. They are listed here as follows:

Diagon Alley
Knockturn Alley
Horizont Alley
Carkitt Market

Diagon Alley Attractions

On Diagon Alley, you will find several iconic

establishments open for business, offering meals, souvenirs, apparel and magical beverages. There are also many businesses with sealed entrances. These establishments have proprietors who have chosen not to conduct business with muggles so they are strictly decorative storefronts. However, there is magic to be found in these shop windows.

Listed below are businesses which are open to muggles.

The Leaky Cauldron

Hagrid's favorite pub, The Leaky Cauldron, is open to muggles from all over the world. Breakfast, lunch and dinner are served at this fine establishment. This restaurant offers the most authentic standards of British pub fare such as Fish & Chips, Toad in the Hole and Bangers & Mash. There is also a Kids Menu and Desserts. For more information, refer to Chapter 11, Fantastic Eats and Where to Find Them.

Madam Malkin's Robes for all Occasions

Wizard robes, Hogwarts house sweaters, scarves, gloves, sweatshirts, backpacks and accessories in all house colors are available for sale in this shop. Notice the mannequins featuring dress robes worn by Celestina Warbeck, Kingsley Shacklebolt, Dumbledore and best of all, Hermione's Yule Ball gown. Most Harry Potter Geeks love the experience of being fitted for their own Hogwarts house robes.

Wink: *The Mirror at Madam Malkin's often offers fashion advice to muggles who stop to gaze at their reflection—sometimes the mirror's observations are not so very polite!*

Shutterbutton's Photography Studio

One form of magic that muggles are entranced by is moving wizard photography. At Shutterbutton's, muggles can create a digital and DVD photo album featuring themselves in 12 different iconic scenes from the Wizarding World. A wizard or witch team member will usher clients into small green screen room decorated in a vintage steampunk style. They will then be given suggestions as to how to behave in each scene while being photographed. When completed, the team member will preview the scenes and offer the DVD for purchase. Shutterbutton's photo sessions are NOT included in My Universal Photos packages.

Quality Quidditch Supplies

Sports fans will love Ron Weasley's favorite shop. Quality Quidditch Supplies is located across the lane from the Leaky Cauldron and next to Weasley's Wizard Wheezes near the entrance to Diagon Alley. Quidditch jerseys, broomsticks, bludgers, golden snitches and a variety of Ravenclaw, Hufflepuff, Slytherin and Gryffindor practice uniforms and apparel may be purchased here. This shop also carries t-shirts flaunting the emblems of your favorite international Quidditch teams.

Weasley's Wizard Wheezes

Giggles abound in this whimsical joke shop founded by Fred and George Weasley. Its storefront is one of the icons of the area with George's top hat lifting to reveal a magic rabbit. It is one of the first iconic sights to encounter when entering Diagon Alley.

The interior is a feast for the eyes with many whimsical items for sale such as Extendable Ears, U No Poo, Puking Pastilles, and Sneak-o-scopes. Look up to see Weasley magical fireworks and a miniature Delores Umbridge tightroping on a unicycle. While it appears to be a two or three story shop, only the first floor is accessible to muggles.

Popular souvenir items at Weasley's:

Extendable Ears
Cycling Dolores Umbridge
Pygmy Puffs
Screaming Yo Yo
Boxing Telescope

Popular edibles treats at Weasley's:

Fever Fudge
U No Poo
Puking Pastilles
Fainting Fancies
Nosebleed Nougat

Wizard Trivia Question No. 4: What pet did Jenny choose from her brothers' shop to take to Hogwarts as her pet and what did she name it?

Ollivanders

No visit to Diagon Alley is complete without a visit to Ollivanders to take part in "The Wand Chooses the Wizard" ceremony. During each visit to Ollivanders, one visitor is chosen to test a wand with a few spells and have a wand choose them. After the ceremony, guests exit through Ollivanders Wand Shop where you may choose your favorite wand which may or may not be a replica of one that belonged to one of your favorite characters. Notice details around the shop like the Celtic Tree Calendar on the wall representing the different wand materials. Ollivanders has absolutely the best personal service in Diagon Alley.

Tip: New collectible wands are issued each year.

Wink: *Should your interactive wand get broken, bring it back to Ollivanders and they will take it in the back to "magically" repair it. This service is also available at Owl Post in Hogsmeade.*

Florean Fortescue's Ice Cream Parlour

As the Florida heat intensifies, a stop in at Harry's favorite ice cream parlour is exactly what Madame Pomfrey ordered. Florean's offers a uniquely delicious array of flavours in both soft serve and hard packed ice creams. The showpiece flavour is ButterBeer Ice Cream which is a striped soft serve delight. Other popular flavours include Chocolate Chili, Earl Grey and Lavender, Sticky Toffee Pudding, and Harry's favorite, Strawberry Peanutbutter. For more information, refer to Chapter 11, Fantastic Eats and Where to Find Them.

Knockturn Alley Attractions

A visit to Diagon Alley would not be complete without a venture into this dark arts corridor. Barely visible to muggles (and Hufflepuffs for that matter), the entrance to Knockturn Alley is just beyond The Leaky Cauldron. A second entrance is located next to the Fountain of Fair Fortune. Notice the chill in the air as your eyes adjust to the darkness when you enter this lane—a wonderful escape from the high heat of Florida. Knockturn Alley has lots of opportunities to cast some of the most imaginative spells in the area.

Wink: The sky in this area is enchanted like the great hall in Hogwarts Castle. However, in Knockturn Alley, it is perpetually a night sky.

Wink: Test all of the door knobs in Knockturn Alley if you dare!

Borgin and Burkes

The only shop open to muggles in Knockturn Alley is an attraction and a shop combined. Skulls, Death Eater masks, dark magic items and apparel are available for purchase. There are several dark magic items on display in the shop from the books and films including the Vanishing Cabinet from *Harry Potter and the Half Flood Prince*, the cursed opal necklace meant for Dumbledore as well as the Hand of Glory which grabbed Harry in *Harry Potter and the Chamber of Secrets*.

Horizont Alley Attractions

Horizont Alley is a very short lane but with the main distinction of being home to Gringotts Wizarding Bank. The iconic bank building is home to the popular ride, Harry Potter and the Escape from Gringotts.

Harry Potter and the Escape from Gringotts

Goblins and wizards collaborated to bring to Diagon Alley its feature attraction. This is another which is two attractions in one. Tour the bank and then ride through the caverns. Gringotts has an elegant and extensive queue which takes muggle guests on a tour through the great lobby of Gringotts Wizarding Bank, which is virtually identical to what you see when Harry Potter visited the bank with Hagrid in *Harry Potter and the Sorcerer's Stone.*

Upon starting your tour, the very strict Gringotts security guards will direct you through the grand lobby with its crystal chandeliers, marble columns and gold gilt ornate finishes. The unfriendly clerks occasional glance up and obviously don't approve of this intrusion of muggles. These goblins are in fact a product of muggle ingenuity better known as audio animatronic engineering. The head goblin, Bogrod, who sits upon the raised podium gives instructions on how to enter a vault.

The queue then takes guests to the interior of the bank through an office hallway, passing a number goblin offices, to Bill Weasley's office. After an introduction by Bill, guests enter the "lift" in which riders "descend" miles down into the cavernous underground depths to access vault carts.

At the cart loading station, riders load into carts which have three rows which accommodate four riders to each row. After riders put on 3-D glasses, four inter-connected carts launch on the journey through the caverns of Gringotts depths.

The journey starts out on a metal roller coaster track, but this is no ordinary roller coaster ride. Be prepared for a multi-dimensional experience. You will spin, go backwards, have sudden stops, and have high speed chases. On this ride, you will encounter troll guards, a couple of dark wizards including "He who must not be named," a dragon and even our favorite trio, Harry, Ron and Hermione.

The cast of Harry Potter and the Escape from Gringotts film sequences includes several actors reprising their roles from the films:

Helena Bonham Carter as Bellatrix Lestrange

Ralph Fiennes as Lord Voldemort
Domhnall Gleeson as Bill Weasley
Rupert Grint as Ron Weasley
Daniel Radcliffe as Harry Potter
Emma Watson, Hermione Granger

Riders must be 42 inches tall, and all loose articles and bags must be stowed in the free temporary lockers. This ride is less "scary" and more friendly to those who experience motion sickness than the original Harry Potter ride in the castle in Hogsmeade.

Wink: *Riding in the last row of the cart is a bit more thrilling. There is less leg room in the front cart.*

Wizard Trivia Question No. 5: What is the name of the goblin who takes Harry and Hagrid to his vault on his first to Gringotts Bank?

Globus Mundi

This shop in Diagon Alley has the back story of a Wizarding World Travel Agency for wizards and witches. The walls are covered with posters of places where wizards wish to travel. There is a variety of merchandise at this establishment for sale including Hogwarts Express themed merchandise, luggage and Globus Mundi Tumblers. This shop may be closed during days with low attendance.

The Fountain of Fair Fortune

Named after the famous story from *The Tales of Beedle the Bard,* this is a quick service stop to purchase both non-alcoholic and alcoholic beverages. The most popular beverages are Butterbeer as well as other magical offerings including a refreshing Fishy Green Ale, Otter Fizzy Orange, Fire Whiskey or try a brew exclusive to Diagon—Wizards'

Brew or Dragon Scale. For more information, refer to Chapter 11, Fantastic Eats and Where to Find Them.

Magical Menagerie

All of the magical beasts in the Wizarding World are available as plushes in this shop. Available for purchase are plush Hedwig owl puppets, phoenix, scaly creatures and lots of other plush creatures. Look up to see Luna's favorite beast, the triple horned Snorkak.

Wink: *While everyone assumes the big snake in the window is Voldemort's snake, Nagini, they may be correct. However, there are two snakes in the window! The second may be the snake which Harry released from the zoo in Harry Potter and the Sorcerer's Stone.*

Wiseacre's Wizarding Equipment

Most guests enter this shop while exiting Harry Potter and the Escape from Gringotts. Stop to browse this interesting shop if you are looking for Hogwarts Express shirts and merchandise. Inside you will find all sorts of wizarding world of Harry Potter merchandise including apparel, magnifying glasses, crystal balls, telescopes, ornaments and more.

Scribbulus

At Scribbulus, a Hogwarts student or a visiting muggle can find stationary, assorted feather quills, backpacks, journals, lanyards and even howlers with Hogwarts house insignias.

Carkitt Market Area Attractions

The Carkitt Market area resembles some of London's quaint markets, however there is more to do than just shop. Listed below is what you may find at Carkitt Market:

Gringotts Money Exchange

In this small office near the Harry Potter and the Escape from Gringotts attraction, muggles may direct questions to the attending goblin clerk and receive grumpy responses, take selfies and exchange muggle U. S. currency for Gringotts bank notes to keep as souvenirs or spend in the theme parks. Gringotts merchandise is also for sale.

Eternelle's Elixir of Refreshment

At this kiosk, Gilly Water (bottled water) is sold along with a choice of four different flavored elixirs which can be added to water to quench your thirst. For more information, refer to Chapter 11, Fantastic Eats and Where to Find Them.

Wink: *Look up at Eternelle's and notice the different fantastic beasts at each corner of this kiosk.*

The Hopping Pot

This is a outdoor pub style bar with counter service. The menu has lots of magical themed beverages and snacks. There are picnic tables which offer a great view of the alternating shows performed in Carkitt Market. For more information, refer to Chapter 11, Fantastic Eats and Where to Find Them.

Mermaid Statue

One of the most popular spell casting spots in Diagon Alley is the Mermaid Statue, inspired from the film, *Harry*

Potter and the Goblet of Fire. Many an unsuspecting muggle gets wet from this spewing fountain!

Celestina Warbeck and the Banshees

At the Diagon Alley stage, everyone can enjoy the jazzy, musical stylings from the "singing sorceress," Celestina Warbeck, the long time favorite of Molly Weasley. Along with the Banshees, Ms. Warbeck entertains and occasionally calls a muggle up to perform with her!

The Tales of Beedle the Bard

Yet another Confundus Curse must have been placed when J. K. Rowling was allowed to publish *The Tales of Beedle the Bard* in book form. These tales became famous with muggles in the book and film, *Harry Potter and the Deathly Hallows*. In Carkitt Market, elaborate puppet shows of the two most famous tales entertain muggles each day at alternating times. Performance times vary, but *The Tale of the Three Brothers* and *The Fountain of Fair Fortune* puppet shows are performed every 45 minutes or so. Showtimes may be reduced on days with lower park attendance.

Wands by Gregorovitch

Dumbledore's Slytherin House contemporary, Mykew Gregorovitch's wand shop is managed at Diagon Alley by a few of Gregorovitch's contemporaries. At this legendary wand maker's stand, muggles may choose from an assortment of interactive wands available for purchase, but visit Ollivanders for more variety of wands.. This shop may be closed on days with lower attendance.

Wink: *Gregorovitch wands are favored by students from the House of Slytherin.*

Owl Post

At Owl Post, muggles may have their purchases boxed, tied and shipped in brown paper packaging with an Own Post stamp just like those which are delivered by owls to Hogwarts students. Packages may be shipped anywhere in the continental United States.

Sugarplum's Sweet Shop

At Sugarplum's Sweet Shop, muggles can satisfy their sweet tooth with the sweetest confections of the wizarding world. Sugarplums carries almost every type of sweet available at Honeydukes in Hogsmeade. Every nook is stocked with colorful sweets and tasty temptations sure to satisfy even the most traditional muggles. Choose from Exploding Bon Bons, Acid Pops, Pepper Imps, Pink Coconut Ice or my favorite, Peppermint Chocolate Toads. Also found in the glass bakery case are baked treats like Cauldron Cakes, Pumpkin Pasties and a variety of fudge with the most popular being Butterbeer Fudge. On occasion, chocolate frog cards can be traded with the clerk.

"I hope you're pleased with yourselves. We could all have been killed — or worse, expelled."
Hermione Granger
Harry Potter and the Sorcerer's Stone

CHAPTER 6: THE VILLAGE OF HOGSMEADE

The original installment of the The Wizarding World of Harry Potter was the village of Hogsmeade at Universal's Islands of Adventure. With Universal Orlando's attention to detail, the iconic Hogwarts Castle and J. K. Rowling's creative control, this immersive land continues to draw visitors who want to experience the magic of Hogwarts Castle. In Hogsmeade, you can ride an enchanted bench or a magical motorbike, and do such things as cast spells, mail a post card with a Hogsmeade postmark or listen to a whinging ghost in the loo. After all of these years, guests are still discovering new details at this enchanted destination.

Hogsmeade Attractions

Hagrid's Magical Creatures Motorbike Adventure

On Hagrid's Magical Creatures Motorbike Adventure you fly far beyond the grounds of Hogwarts castle through the Forbidden Forest on a thrilling roller coaster ride that plunges guests into the paths of some of the wizarding world's rarest magical creatures. The ride has a fantastic queue with several *Winks* from the wizarding world and past attractions at this location, along with ground breaking and exciting elements found on no other coaster!

Warning: Spoilers!

After proceeding through the immersive queue, full of Winks, you enter the motorbike ride vehicles on a moving platform (alert a team member if you need to slow it down). The ride vehicle is a motorbike and side car with a lap bar. It is not required to hold the handlebars while riding the motorbike but some say it enhances the experience. As you begin the ride, Hagrid casts spells which go awry causing sudden bursts of speed, backward motion, and even a vertical drop! On the ride you'll will encounter a Centaur, a Blast Ended Skrewt (this creature was only found in the books), a Hagrid animatronic figure, as well as the Weasley's enchanted Ford Anglia and a Unicorn with her foal.

Hagrid's ride has been proclaimed by many to be the most fun ride in Orlando, it has attracted record crowds willing to wait sometimes more than three hours to ride. On occasion, the ride is only available by Virtual line access which requires use of the Universal Orlando app. This causes a problem for inexperienced guests. A call to Universal Orlando Guest Services at 407-224-4233 should give the most up-to-date information on ride access. Email Universal Orlando at GuestServices@UniversalOrlando.com. If you are unable to gain access to the ride, visit the Guest Services location near Hogsmeade Station.

Wizard Trivia Question No. 6: What are the four houses of Ilvermorny Academy, located in the United States?

Harry Potter and the Forbidden Journey

The centerpiece of Hogsmeade is the iconic Hogwarts Castle which can be seen from miles away. The castle is home to what you may consider two attractions in one. In Harry Potter and the Forbidden Journey, the walk through the queue is your "castle tour." The second part of the attraction is a four minute multi-sensory, multi-dimensional. The ride "vehicle," an enchanted bench, uses a ground breaking muggle invention, Kuka-Arm technology, which is similar to a giant "hand" carrying each bench and follows a track. It tips riders backwards, forwards and swings around in all directions. This award winning ride gives you the sensation of flying. The ride, however, is not recommended for those who suffer with motion sickness or Vertigo.

The Castle Tour

Warning: If you hate spoilers, read no more about the castle tour and ride!

For muggles who do not wish to board the ride for health reasons, the Castle Tour is the best way to discover and enjoy the secrets of Hogwarts Castle. When the attraction opened, a Hogwarts Student would be your tour guide upon request. These days, however, guests follow the queue until they reach the boarding station. A team member will advise you how to exit or wait in the Child Swap Family Room while others in your party ride. The attraction begins with the back story of guests joining a group of muggles to attend a lecture on the history of Hogwarts Castle, but end up in a Quidditch match.

Follow the tour by entering in the Dungeons. On your right is the statue of the hump-backed witch—which marks the entrance to the underground tunnel into Honeydukes of which we learned the existence of in *Harry Potter and the Prisoner of Azkaban*. On your left, you will notice the Mirror of Erised and the Potions Classroom door. If you look closely you might notice Professor Snape's office near the hump backed witch. As you continue on, you will pass through the greenhouses where Hogwarts students study Herbology.

The queue leads back into the castle through a corridor with a gold statue of the architect of Hogwarts Castle—he is holding a model in his right hand. Located next to the statue are the four jewel glass vessels which mark the progress for the Hogwarts House Cup (Harry's house, Gryffindor, is in the lead, of course). The next statue is the first headmaster of Hogwarts and then we see the gold Gryphon statue which marks the entrance to Professor Dumbledore's office.

As the tour continues, we come to a favorite place of mine, the portrait gallery along a staircase. Among others, likenesses of the four founders of Hogwarts have been captured in portraits and are having a heated discussion concerning the muggles touring the castle. Of course, Salazar Slytherin is disturbed by the onlooking muggles.

Wink: It is best to do the castle tour in the early hours or when the wait time is low.

Wizard Trivia Question No. 7 What does the Mirror of Erised's inscription say?

We pass through to Dumbledore's office and meet the

great wizard, himself as he warns of a dragon on the loose. The next stop is the Dark Arts classroom. You will want to proceed slowly through this room because there are so many details to see. Notice the dragon skeleton above. While in the classroom, we are interrupted by Harry, Ron and Hermione who invite you to a Quidditch match!

Guests are then directed to the Gryffindor Common Room where they meet The Fat Lady's portrait, who guards the entrance and isn't happy about letting in muggles into the Gryffindor Common Room without a password! Further along is the famous Sorting Hat on a shelf to the right who gives instructions on boarding the ride once you reach the Room of Requirement. As the Sorting Hat says, "You must be more than Goblin size, at least 48 inches tall to ride." The Room of Requirement is where muggles board enchanted benches on a moving platform. This is end of the Castle Tour. Speak to a Team Member who will advise you how to exit the castle.

Wink: *The same statue of the hump-backed witch at the castle entrance is first seen in the film, Harry Potter and the Sorcerer's Stone, in the scene just before Ron, Harry, and Hermione find Hagrid's three headed dog, Fluffy.*

Wizard Trivia Question No. 8: Where did Tom Riddle's parents meet?

The Forbidden Journey

As you enter the Room of Requirement, you are actually entering the loading platform for the ride. This is a moving platform which means the ride vehicles are in constant motion. This moving platform moves quite quickly. The attendants can direct you to a stationary platform if you need assistance boarding.

The attendant will secure a shoulder harness in place on

your enchanted bench before the ride begins. There are test seats at the entrance if you are unsure if you will fit. There are no loops on this ride, but it does tip you backwards and almost upside down at one point. Guests feet will dangle on this ride so appropriate footwear should be worn. Many a muggle has lost a flip flop sandal on the ride, causing a temporary shutdown.

The journey begins as Hermione casts a spell and enchants the bench which sends guests through the Floo Network. You are then met by Harry and Ron on broomsticks and your bench follows them to a Quidditch Match. Guests meet Hagrid on the way who is looking for an escaped dragon. You come face to face with the dragon and are chased into the dark and scary Forbidden Forest where you will experience dragon breath and other scary things such as giant spiders and the Whomping Willow.

With Hermione's help you head back to the Quidditch Pitch where you are chased by Dementors into the Chamber of Secrets. At this point, you will encounter the terrifying Basilisk and Dementors. Harry casts the Expecto Patronum spell just as you are about to receive the Dementor's Kiss and you escape back to celebrate Gryffindor's victory! Dumbledore sends you traveling back through the Floo Network to exit the ride. After exiting, you end up at Filch's Emporium of Confiscated Goods to shop for a few themed items and retrieve your belonging from the temporary lockers.

The filmed sequences in Harry Potter and the Forbidden Journey features actors who were cast as the same characters of the film series including:

Daniel Radcliffe as Harry Potter
Emma Watson as Hermione Granger
Rupert Grint as Ron Weasley
Michael Gambon as Albus Dumbledore

Robbie Coltrane as Rubeus Hagrid
Tom Felton as Draco Malfoy
Mathew Lewis as Neville Longbottom
Bonnie Wright as Ginny Weasley
James Phelps as Fred Weasley
Oliver Phelps as George Weasley
Warwick Davis as Professor Flitwick

Guests are not permitted to bring any bags or loose items on this attraction. Free temporary lockers are available as you enter the dungeons, but using one of these lockers can be a scene of chaos on a busy day.

Wink: *As you enter the enchanted bench, look up at the ceiling.*

Wink: *While riding look down and to the left under the Whomping Willow to see a broken Enchanted Bench!*

Ollivanders™

Ollivanders is a maker of fine wands since 382 B.C. Mr. Ollivander opened this new location at Hogsmeade in 2010. He misjudged, however, how many muggles would stand in line to step into the small dusty shop with wand boxes stacked to the ceiling for their chance to be chosen at the Wand Chooses the Wizard Ceremony. The wait time can be quite long at this location without the benefit of much shade in the queue. After the show, you may choose from a selection of wands including Harry Potter film character wands, collectible wands, interactive wands and replica wands. Many guests opt for the very similar Ollivanders experience at the location in Diagon Alley which has more space.

Hogwarts Express: Hogsmeade Station

When guests are ready to depart Hogsmeade and travel back to London and Diagon Alley, the best mode of travel is the Hogwarts Express: Hogsmeade Station. A Hogwarts Prefect will guide your party to a compartment aboard the Hogwarts Express. As you depart, while gazing through your compartment's "window," you'll encounter the irrepressible Weasley twins on broomstick advertising their shop in Diagon Alley. After admiring the scenic views of the British countryside from the train window, it won't be long before you get a glimpse of the Knight Bus before arriving at your London destination, Kings Cross Station.

Flight of the Hippogriff

Flight of the Hippogriff is a family-friendly, small roller coaster based upon everyone's favorite feathered character, Buckbeak. The actual coaster ride is very short, but what makes it worth the wait are the views of Hogsmeade seen from the ride and the charming queue featuring Hagrid's cabin. The ride is a great choice for those too small or timid to ride Hagrid's Magical Creatures Motorbike Adventure. The coaster is just fast enough to be fun for all ages. As you ascent the first hill remember to show the proper respect and bow to Buckbeak who is sitting in his nest!

Wink: *This is the only remaining re-designed attraction from the original section of the Lost Continent from which the Wizarding World was created. The former attraction from the Lost Continent was called The Flying Unicorn.*

You must be 36 inches in height to ride. This family friendly ride is classified as a roller coaster and your seat is secured by a lap bar.

Wizard Trivia Question No. 9: What was the new name

given to Buckbeak, the Hippogriff, when he was given back to Hagrid after Sirius' death?

Hogsmeade Refreshments

The Three Broomsticks

In the book, *Harry Potter and the Prisoner of Azkaban,* Harry sneaks into Hogsmeade and sits in the back of the Three Broomsticks. It is in this same place that he develops his love for the tasty beverage—Butterbeer. This restaurant was actually completed before the third film was completed so the film sets were almost identical to the theme of this establishment. The atmosphere is complete with vaulted ceilings flanked by oak beams and dark furniture which has seen lots of magic. If the weather is nice, additional seating is available outside overlooking the lake but the magic may be broken with a view of the VelociCoaster. Additional seating is also available in the adjacent Hogs Head Pub—a good place to order an adult beverage.

The menu is consists of hearty British fare as well as park favorites from the previous Lost Continent restaurant which stood on this spot, the Enchanted Oak Tavern. Fish and chips, Shepherd's pie (Harry's favorite), Beef Pasties, roasted chicken, chargrilled ribs, smoked turkey legs, fresh vegetables and desserts complete the lunch and dinner menu. The restaurant also features a hearty breakfast menu. For more information, see Chapter 11: Fantastic Eats and Where to Find Them.

Wink: *Where in the world is Sirius Black? Although he has been one of the most prominent people in the life of Harry Potter, he is hard to find in the wizarding world. You may purchase his wand or a Padfoot plush dog, but where can you find him? He is featured in a wanted poster near the Three Broomsticks.*

Wink: The Three Broomsticks sign loosely represents the symbol for the Deathly Hallows.

Hog's Head Pub

At the rear of the Three Broomsticks tavern is the Hog's Head Pub. The whole family is welcome in the authentic pub where many enjoy Harry's favorite beverage, Butterbeer. Other drinks include pumpkin juice, lemonade, and cider. Adults may order at the bar and sample the pub's selection of domestic and imported beers on tap, specialty drinks, wine, spirits and mixed drinks including Hagrid's favorite, Fire Whisky.

Wink: Look out for the large stuffed hog's head behind the bar which occasionally snarls at guests.

Butterbeer Keg Cart

One of the single most popular items at the wizarding world is Butterbeer. A Butterbeer from one of the large red kegs is a rite of passage for muggles visiting The Wizarding World of Harry Potter. The lines have been so long at this cart that a second cart was added to Hogsmeade. At this cart, you can purchase three varieties—the original, frozen Butterbeer and Hot Butterbeer.

The Magic Neep

Another open kiosk, the Magic Neep is geared to muggles who desire a healthy snack or beverage. This open air cart offers guests fresh fruits on ice, cold bottled water and snacks to refresh and nourish in the hot Florida climate. If you look behind it, you can see the Magic Neep store front.

Filch's Emporium of Confiscated Goods

As you exit the Forbidden Journey, you are directed through a shop inspired by the perpetually cranky caretaker, Mr. Filch. As the name implies, this shop has a variety of items for purchase, such as Hogwarts and Quidditch clothing, toys, movie prop replicas, and another great example of "Muggle Magic," the Interactive Marauders Map, which includes a wand for use only on the map. Also in this shop, at the attraction's exit, guests can purchase a photo of their ride experience.

Wink: The Hogwarts Students employed at Filch's shop are all on detention. Ask them for what reason they got a detention!

Dervish and Banges

Before the opening of Diagon Alley, muggles desiring wizarding and Quidditch equipment had only one shop to explore. Dervish and Banges is still providing a wide range of magical supplies and wizarding equipment such as Sneakoscopes, Spectrespecs, Omnioculars, and wands. See The Monster Book of Monsters on display. If you are shopping for Quidditch supplies, Dervish and Bangs carries t-shirts, Quaffles, Golden Snitches and brooms including the Nimbus Two Thousand and One and the Firebolt. Hogwarts school uniforms and clothing including robes, scarves, ties, t-shirts and sweatshirts are also available at this store.

Wizard Trivia Question No. 10: Where did Harry Potter take Cho Chang on a date?

Honeydukes

A favorite of muggles and wizards is Hogsmeade's legendary sweetshop, Honeydukes. The shelves are lined with colorful sweets, including Acid Pops, Fizzing Whizzbees, Peppermint Toads and the very popular, Chocolate Frogs. Brave muggles love to try Bertie Bott's Every-Flavour Beans with tasty (and not so tasty) flavours to discover!

Chocolate frogs are popular with collectors for the collectible Wizard cards in each box. The card collecting started with only four, the founders of Hogwarts, before more were added. Here is a list of the available Chocolate Frog Cards:

Godric Gryffindor—Founder of Gryffindor House
Rowena Ravenclaw—Founder of Ravenclaw House
Helga Hufflepuff—Founder of Hufflepuff House
Salazar Slytherin—Founder of Slytherin House
Albus Dumbledore—particularly famous for his defeat of the Dark Wizard Grindelwald.
Gilderoy Lockhart—Wizarding Celebrity Author
Hengist of Woodcroft—founder of the Village of Hogsmeade
Bertie Bott—Creator of Bertie Bott's Every-Flavour Beans
Jocunda Sykes—the first witch to fly over the Atlantic by broom.
Devlin Whitehorn—known for creating the Nimbus Racing Broom Company.

Wink: *In 2014, an Undetectable Extension charm was placed on Honeydukes as the inside was expanded to take over the inside space of Zonko's Joke Shop which closed when the Weasleys' shop opened in Diagon Alley.*

Geek Tip: Chocolate Frogs are often bought as souvenirs. The high quality chocolate is formulated so that it doesn't melt quickly but ask a Team Member if your purchase can be sent to the park exit or your onsite hotel to ensure its safety until you are ready to exit the park.

Owl Post

Owl Post sells wands, stationery, Hogsmeade stamps, postcards, writing implements, owl plush toys and gifts. What attracts many muggles to this shop is the ability to send letters and packages in wizarding world wrapping (for a fee) with a special Hogsmeade™ postmark—a cool souvenir (you may bring your own stamps and stationery for mailing letters).

Hogsmeade Entertainment

On the open air stage located near Flight of the Hippogriff, alternating shows are performed inspired by several of the Harry Potter films.

The Frog Choir

A Hogwarts student announces The Frog Choir, an a-cappella singing group composed of four Hogwarts student singers and two singing frogs. The singing group is inspired by a scene in the film, *Harry Potter and the Prisoner of Azkaban.*

During the ten minute show, the group performs popular wizard favorites such as *Something Wicked This Way Comes* and *Hedwig's Theme.* The singers and frogs are available for photographs after the performance. Holiday tunes are added during the Christmas season.

The Triwizard Spirit Rally

Inspired by the film, *Harry Potter and the Goblet of*

Fire, the Triwizard Spirit Rally is an exciting pep rally. The young men of Durmstrang Institute perform in an athletically acrobatic style, as they perform a coordinated routine with sticks, kicks and jumps to the Durmstrang theme. Next, the lovely ladies of Beauxbatons Academy of Magic arrive in their blue traveling cloaks to perform in a choreographed performance with batons and ribbons to their own lovely themed music.

"Oh, these people's minds work in strange ways, Petunia, they're not like you and me," said Uncle Vernon, trying to knock in a nail with the piece of fruitcake Aunt Petunia had just brought him."
Vernon Dursley
Harry Potter and the Sorcerer's Stone

CHAPTER 7: MUGGLES MAKING MAGIC

Wizards and witches throughout the world are still astounded at the reversal of past standards of secrecy for the practice of magic in the presence of muggles. Nevertheless, muggles are allowed to practice a limited amount of magic with interactive wands at Universal Orlando. The portraits in Dumbledore's office have certainly had much discussion of the merits or disastrous effects this decision will have. Salazar Slytherin's portrait is perpetually disturbed at the sight of all these muggles using wands!

With interactive wands, muggles may cast simple spells at specific locations with delightful effects. Character wands are available which match the wand of the most popular characters from the films such as Harry, Hermione, Dumbledore and even the original wand of "He Who Must Not Be Named!" There are also many styles of "unclaimed" wands waiting to choose their wizards. Mr. Ollivander is still busy because several new limited edition collectible wands became available for purchase in 2023.

Wizard Trivia Question No. 11: Which Hogwarts professor is neither a witch nor a wizard?

Wink: *The old "replica" wands are still for sale at a lower price than the interactive wands. These collectible wands cost about $50 while the interactive wands cost about $60 or more.*

Visiting Ollivander's shop in Diagon Alley is the best way for muggles to purchase a wand but also to learn information about wand lore. Ollivander's wands correspond to the Celtic Tree Calendar, as seen on the wall of the shop.

Wink: *J. K. Rowling linked Harry, Ron and Hermione's wand to the Celtric Tree calendar and now you can have this link too. Tell the team members at Ollivander's your birthday and they will tell you which wand wood to purchase.*

Wands are also available Ollivander's in Hogsmeade, at Wands by Gregorovitch in Diagon Alley, at the Universal Stores in CityWalk and Universal Studios, at onsite hotel gift shops and on the Universal Orlando website. If you have the luxury of time, get your wand at Ollivanders in Diagon Alley.

Included with your interactive wand is a two-sided and very collectible map of the Wizarding World with spell locations. These maps lead you to brass medallion markers in the pavement which point to the spot of each spell. On the medallions as well as on the map is a diagram of how the spell should be cast.

***Wink:** There are secrets on your Spell Map which can only be revealed under the black light in Knockturn Alley.*

***Wink:** Diagon Alley is open during Halloween Horror Nights, a curious Dark Arts event for the purpose of scaring muggles. This is a great time to visit Diagon Alley, ride Harry Potter and the Escape from Gringotts and also to cast spells!*

Casting Spells in The Wizarding World– Diagon Alley

Provided for you here is a list of magic spell locations with the corresponding spells to study before visiting Diagon Alley. This list does not intend to spoil the surprise of magic, but rather to prepare muggles for their first attempt at magic. The spells have slightly varied difficulty levels, but there is usually a wizard team member nearby to assist. Muggles get better at spell casting with practice. Because of the crowded conditions of Diagon Alley and Hogsmeade, knowing where to look for spells before your visit will be very helpful. Muggles spell casting abilities improve with practice. If you have acquired a wand prior to your visit, it is a good idea to study the map which is included.

Tips to help with Spell Casting:

- Arrive at the park opening time to cast spells in less crowded conditions.

- Stand directly behind the spell brass medallion.

- Hold your arm straight out at the target and flick your wand from the wrist instead of swinging your arms.

- Ask a Wizard Team Member for help if you have difficulty achieving magic.

Horizont Alley Spell Locations

- Pilliwinkle's Playthings, Spell: Tarantallegra

- Flimflams Lanterns, Spell: Incendio

- Umbrella Sign, Spell: Meteolojinx

- Magical Menagerie, Spell: Silencio

- Wiseacres Wizarding Equipment, Spell: Dark Detectors

- Wiseacres Wizarding Equipment, Spell: Specialis Revelio

- Scribbulus, Spell: Wingardium Leviosa

Secret Spell Location—Scribbulus: In the window to the right of the Scribbulus shop door

Carkitt Market Spell Locations

- Brown E. Wright Blacksmith, Spell: Reparo

- Brown E. Wright Blacksmith, Spell: Locomotor Bellows

- Mermaid Fountain, Spell: Aguamenti

Diagon Alley Spell Locations

Weasley's Wizard Wheezes, Spell: Descendio

Secret Spell Location—There are two secret spell locations at Slug and Jigger's Apothecary

- In the Slug & Jiggers Apothecary window along Diagon Alley. This one is not so secret anymore. The pile of dragon dung spell location is on the new wand maps, but it does not have a medallion on the ground in front, so it can still be considered a secret for those without a map.

- In the Slug & Jiggers Apothecary window along Diagon Alley (to the right of the prior spell)

Casting Spells in Knockturn Alley

- Chimney Sweep Elf Sign, Spell: Locomotor Chimney Sweep

- Dystyl Phaelanges, Spell: Moving Skeleton

- Noggin and Bonce, Spell: Mimblewimble

- Tallow and Hemp Toxic Tapers, Spell: Incendio

- Trackleshanks Locksmith, Spell: Alohomora

Casting Spells in The Wizarding World– Hogsmeade

Because Hogsmeade was originally built without the ability to cast spells, the modifications and the lack of space in throughout makes spell casting in Hogsmeade a little more difficult, but just as magical.

- Zonko's Joke Shop, Spell: Incendio

- McHavelocks, Spell: Arresto Momentum

- Honeyduke's, Spell: Revelio

- Dogweed and Deathcap, Spell: Herbivicus

- Gladrags Wizardwear, Spell: Asecendio/ Descendio

- Madam Puddifoots, Spell: Locomotor Snowman

- Dervish and Banges, Spell: Locomotor – Arresto Momentum

- Tome and Scrolls, Spell: Alohomora

- Spintwitches, Spell: Wingardium Leviosa

'He was a skinny, black-haired, bespectacled boy who had the pincer, slightly unhealthy look of someone who has grown a lot in a short space of time.'
Harry Potter and the Order of the Phoenix

CHAPTER 8: A WIZARD'S JOURNEY THROUGH BOOKS AND FILMS

Muggles and fans of the Harry Potter series of books always express their delight at the first sight of the Wizarding World of Harry Potter. In this chapter, we will follow Harry's footsteps as he experienced the magic and wonders of Diagon Alley and Hogsmeade for the first time. Follow these directions to recreate Harry Potter's journey into the world of magic.

FYI: This journey is more closely related to locations in the books which have been documented with more detail than the films.

Embarking on the Magical Journey

To begin your wizard's journey, enter Universal Studios and walk straight through Minion Land to the New York section and turn right when you see the Macy's storefront. Follow this lane through San Francisco all the way to the London waterfront.

In the London Waterfront, you will see Kings Cross Station, a record shop and book shop, Leicester Square Station, the Wyndham Theater, and Grimmauld Place. Look for a nondescript door which looks to be a part of the book shop (muggles usually don't notice it) with the weathered and aged Leaky Cauldron sign. This door represents the entrance to The Leaky Cauldron as described in the book.

In the first book of the series about the famous young wizard, *Harry Potter and the Sorcerer's Stone,* Harry is brought to the Leaky Cauldron by Rubeus Hagrid, Hogwarts Keeper of the Keys.

Entering Diagon Alley

Muggles do not actually enter Diagon Alley through the Leaky Cauldron door in London. Next to the record shop is a red building with the sign that reads "Leicester (pronounced Lester) Square Station." Enter under this sign and you'll soon see the opening in the bricks (the bricks are permanently open so as to prevent muggle heart attacks at their first sight of magic).

Many muggles have the same reaction as Harry Potter at the first sight of Diagon Alley, you will wish you had eight more eyes! It is truly magical with the sights, sounds, and smells of a wizarding village. Many a muggle has been reduced to tears at their first sight of Diagon Alley. In this magical area, you will be immersed in the magical theme which means you won't see any theme park rides or American advertisements.

On your left is the actual muggle entrance to **The Leaky Cauldron**. Harry went to the Leaky Cauldron with Hagrid before entering Diagon Alley so this is your first stop. Step inside and bask in the atmosphere (you may ask one of the Team Members to take a look around).

Exchanging Muggle Currency

Your next stop is Harry Potter and the Escape from Gringotts. The magnificent facade of Gringotts Bank is awe inspiring! Walk straight down the lane as you enter Diagon Alley. It is impossible to miss (curiously, one of Gringotts protection dragons must have gotten loose and is sitting on top of it).

To adhere to Harry's timely journey, you may ask the attendant to tour the ride queue at this time and see the goblin clerks (or visit the ride later). If you want to exchange your muggle dollars, turn right at the bank building and proceed to Gringotts Money Exchange on the left. At this location you may speak to the goblin clerk on duty to exchange your muggle dollars for Gringotts bank notes.

Wink: *Hagrid's motorbike and sidecar is parked next to Gringotts Bank.*

Wizard Trivia Question No. 12: How much is a gold Galleon worth?

Madam Malkin's Robes for All Occasions

At this point in the journey, Harry was fitted for his wizard robes and **Madam Malkin's Robes for All Occasions** is the place to find everything you need to dress like a Hogwarts student. Turn around and head back toward The Leaky Cauldron and enter the purple store front.

Wizard Trivia Question No. 13: For what purpose are horned slugs useful?

There are several stops on Harry Potter's journey that are not open to muggles. The next stop on Harry's journey is across the lane at the green store front of Flourish and Blott's. This is where Hogwarts students buy school text books. The store front of Pottages Cauldron Shop is next to Madam Malkin's with the very tall stack of cauldrons in front where first year students purchase a cauldron for potions class. The Apothecary shop is where Harry purchased his potion ingredients is down the lane a few steps.

Wizard Trivia Question No. 14: In the film, Harry Potter and the Sorcerer's Stone, which two names were on either side of James Potter on the Gryffindor plaque in the trophy case?

No actual cauldrons or potions supplies are for sale in Diagon Alley and Flourish and Blotts is only a store front but it is fascinating to explore all of the store fronts in Diagon Alley.

Magical Menagerie

Eyelops Owl Emporium is where Hagrid purchased Hedwig for Harry's birthday in *Harry Potter and the*

Sorcerer's Stone, but unfortunately, but the Eyelops proprietors have retired. Do not despair because you may purchase your favorite fantastic magical pets in the form of plush owls like Hedwig and Pigwidgeon as well as a variety of other creatures including Crookshanks, Fang, Buckbeak, Fluffy and Scabbers at Magical Menagerie.

Wizard Trivia Question No. 15: Who named Ron Weasley's owl, Pigwidgeon?

The Wand Chooses the Wizard

The most important item that all young wizards and witches are eager to buy is their wand with which to perform magic. Wands are of extreme importance in the wizarding world and finding the right wand is a tricky business. The next stop on this wizard's journey is **Ollivanders**, Makers of Fine Wands since 382 BC. Enter Ollivanders and perhaps you might be chosen for the "wand chooses the wizard ceremony."

As you exit the Ollivanders show, you may purchase an interactive wand if you desire.

All Aboard the Hogwarts Express

With all your school supplies purchased, enter **King's Cross Station.** An attendant is there to greet you and check your Park to Park pass for admission to board. Wind your way through the corridors until you see Platforms 9 and 10. You'll walk straight through a solid brick wall (or at least it will look like it to the muggles behind you) onto Platform 9 ¾. You will feel the same sense of awe that Harry felt at his first glimpse of the Hogwarts Express! Wind your way around the students' trolleys, trunks and owl cages to the boarding lanes, where a Hogwarts Prefect will be waiting to lead you to your passenger compartment.

Wink: Look for Hedwig's cage at Platform 9 ¾.

The Wizards' Academy

Upon arrival at Hogsmeade Station, exit the Hogwarts Express and turn right. Head straight to the iconic Hogwarts Castle. To specifically follow this timeline, tell the attraction attendant that you are only doing the Castle Tour (which is just following along the queue). The ride associated with this attraction has many elements from later books, and we wouldn't want to jump ahead.

Unfortunately there are no boats for first years, so you will begin in the dungeons, go past the gallery of portraits and Dumbledore's office. Eventually you will see the sorting hat which is now located past the Fat Lady's portrait in the Room of Requirement.

In this book, Professor McGonagall issues detention to Harry, Ron, Hermione and Draco Malfoy. The detention to be served in the Forbidden Forest with Hagrid at night to search for an injured unicorn. The Forbidden Forest is portrayed in the attraction, **Hagrid's Magical Creatures Motorbike Adventure,** located in Hogsmeade just a few steps from the castle. This ride takes you past Hagrid's hut and through the forest. The attraction has many elements from the fourth book so you may prefer to wait before riding as the wait times are usually very long.

At the end of the first book, head back to London on the Hogwarts Express to Kings Cross Station.

Wink: Hagrid's cabin is a location on this journey and can be found in two locations—in the ride queues of Flight of the Hippogriff and in the queue of Hagrid's Magical Creatures Motorbike Adventure.

Beware of Knockturn Alley

In the second book, *Harry Potter and the Chamber of Secrets,* Harry is rescued from the Dursley's house by the Weasley brothers in an enchanted Ford Anglia. This car is seen on the ride, Hagrid's Magical Creatures Motorbike Adventure which you may have also ridden.

Harry is brought to the Burrow to spend the rest of his vacation with the Weasley's. Mrs. Weasley enjoys listening to Celestina Warbeck on Wizard Radio. You can enjoy a **Celestina Warbeck and the Banshees** performance later in the Carkitt Market area of Diagon Alley.

When Harry and the Weasley's go to Diagon Alley to purchase school supplies, Harry takes a wrong turn when he travels through the Floo Network for the first time and arrives at **Borgin and Burkes** at **Knockturn Alley.** After entering Diagon Alley, turn left just pass the Leaky Cauldron to enter Knockturn Alley and follow the dark, cold path until you reach the shop. While in the shop, notice the "Hand of Glory" which grabbed Harry! Notice the large cabinet where Harry hid from the Malfoy's.

Luckily, you won't need Hagrid to lead you out of Knockturn Alley. Just follow the path until you see the light of day. Harry's next stop would be to purchase his school supplies in Diagon Alley. He would then head back to London and ride the Hogwarts Express.

While at school, Harry and Ron meet Moaning Myrtle in the girls bathroom. Moaning Myrtle's voice can be heard in the restrooms in Hogsmeade.

Ron and Harry meet Aragog the giant spider in the Forbidden Forest. Aragog as well as other spiders can be seen on the ride, Harry Potter and the Forbidden Journey. You may ride this now, but it will be more effective to wait.

Wizard Trivia Question No. 17: What is Moaning Myrtle's full name?

The third book in the series is *Harry Potter and the Prisoner of Azkaban*. Harry leaves the Dursley's and heads to London on a magical form of transport.

Wizard Travel by Bus

The Knight Bus is a magical form of transport which took Harry on quite a wild ride. It is parked in the London waterfront area. It is a big purple, triple-decker bus straight out of the movie. If you notice strangely dressed muggles speaking to the attendant, these are probably wizards in a poor disguise trying to arrange transport back to London.

After Harry escapes the Dursley's via the Knight Bus, he heads to the Leaky Cauldron where he spends the rest of his summer until school starts. To follow Harry on his wizard's journey, spend some time in Diagon Alley.

One of Harry's favorite shops is **Quality Quidditch Supplies** where you will find everything you will need to play the most popular sport in the wizarding world! Harry went to this shop every day of the summer to view the Firebolt in the shop window.

Beat the Heat with a Sweet Treat

Harry spent every afternoon of his summer in Diagon Alley at Florean Fortescue's Ice Cream Parlour, sitting at a table to do his summer homework. There are no tables for muggles to sit, but try the delicious ice cream.

While in Diagon Alley, Harry purchases his new schoolbooks, one of which is the Monster Book of Monsters. This volume can be seen where Harry purchased it at Florish and Blott's in Diagon Alley, but it can also be seen in a shop window in Hogsmeade and on a table in the queue of Hagrid's Magical Creature Motorbike Adventure.

Next on his journey, Harry heads back to Hogwarts Castle for his third year.

The Darkest of Creatures

Harry Potter has a terrible reaction to the darkest of all magical creatures—Dementors. He encounters these "soul-less" creatures on the Hogwarts Express ride from Kings Cross Station to Hogsmeade. Ride the Hogwarts Express from London if you dare to encounter them. Dementors also chase Harry during a Quidditch match on the ride, Harry Potter and the Forbidden Journey. Now is a good time to ride this attraction.

Turning Time

Professor McGonogall gives Hermione a Time-Turner to use in order to attend more classes. Time Turner necklaces can be found at merchandise kiosks and in some Hogsmeade shops.

Magical Creatures

In this book, Hagrid is promoted to teach Care of Magical Creatures. In class, Harry meets Buckbeak, the hippogriff. Visit Buckbeak on the ride, **Flight of the Hippogriff**.

Wink: *There is a child's wooden hippogriff in the outside queue of Hagrid's ride across from his hut and there is Hippogriff graffiti on the wall of the queue of Hagrid's Magical Creature Motorbike Adventure.*

During the term, the Dark Arts teacher, Professor Remus Lupin, teaches Harry the Expecto Patronum spell to defend himself from the Dementors. To teach Harry, he uses a Bogart which is hiding in a trunk. The next time you find yourself in Knockturn Alley look for the same Bogart trapped in a trunk in Borgin and Burkes.

Marauder's Map

While at school, the Weasley twins gave Harry Potter the Marauders' Map—which they swiped from the Mr. Filch's office. Harry then uses the map to visit Hogsmeade by way of secret passages.

A statue of a hump backed which marks the entrance of the secret passage which can be found in the beginning of the queue for **Harry Potter and the Forbidden Journey** in Hogsmeade. Secret passages are off limits for muggles, but if you want a Marauder's Map, visit **Filch's Emporium of Confiscated Goods** at the base of Hogwarts castle. Magical "interactive" Marauder's Maps may be purchased which let the viewer follow the footsteps of Dumbledore, Snape, Harry, Ron and Hermione.

When Harry emerges from the secret passageway, he finds himself in the delightful haven of sweet delights, **Honeydukes,** which is home to tempting treats which delight wizards tastebuds! Visit Honeydukes in Hogsmeade to purchase some of these tasty sweets.

Under cover of his invisibility cloak, Harry enters the **Three Broomsticks** to listen in on a conversation. In

Hogsmeade, the Three Broomsticks is a dining establishment where you can choose from British delicacies such as Butterbeer, fish and chips, pasties and Harry's favorite, Shepherds Pie.

The TriWizard Tournament

In the fourth book, *Harry Potter and the Goblet of Fire,* Harry joins his friends to attend the wizarding Quidditch World Cup. Visit **Dervish and Banges** in Hogsmeade for Quidditch supplies. More supplies are available at Quality Quidditch Supplies in Diagon Alley. After the Quidditch Cup, the Dark Mark is seen in the sky. There are symbols of the Dark Mark on merchandise in Borgin and Burkes.

Professor Dumbledore welcomes the students of Beauxbatons and Durmstrang to Hogwarts. Watch the **TriWizard Spirit Rally** at the Hogsmeade stage (consult the Universal Orlando app for show times). Dumbledore also introduces Mad Eye Moody as the new Dark Arts teacher. Mad Eye can be seen on the journey to Hogsmeade on the **Hogwarts Express** train ride.

During a Care of Magical Creatures class, Hagrid gives the class an assignment of raising Blast Ended Skrewts. There are many references to the baby skrewts in the queue of Hagrid's ride and a full grown Blast Ended Skrewt is seen alongside Hagrid on the ride. Ride now if you haven't done so.

Harry is chosen as a champion in the Triwizard Tournament. Before the tournament begins, Harry and the other champions are interviewed by Rita Skeeter, a reporter for the Daily Prophet. The Daily Prophet office is in Diagon Alley.

On the attraction, **Harry Potter and the Forbidden Journey** you will come face to face with the dragon from the first challenge of the Triwizard Tournament.

Harry escaped from the dragon with a golden dragon egg which was a clue to the next challenge. In the film, Harry takes the golden egg into the bath where he is met again by Moaning Myrtle. The golden egg as is located in the queue of Hagrid's Creatures Motorbike Adventure. You must look closely at a cabinet to the right of the shelves with dragons eggs.

Wizard Trivia Question No. 18: In the film, *Harry Potter and the Goblet of Fire*, what type of dragon did Cedric Diggory's pull out of the bag?

Hermione is escorted to the Yule Ball by Victor Krum. Hermione's Yule Ball gown is visible in a shop window of Gladrags Wizardwear in Hogsmeade.

Harry meets the king of the Mer people in the underwater challenge. To see the corresponding Mermaid statue, go to Carkitt Market in Diagon Alley (a popular spell location).

Harry stumbles upon the Pensieve in Dumbledore's office. You can see it in the queue of the ride in Hogwarts Castle.

The Home of Black Magic

In book number five, *Harry Potter and the Order of the Phoenix,* Harry leaves the Dursley's with the help of a few aurors. He arrives at Number 12 Grimmauld Place in London, the home of Harry's Godfather, Sirius Black, which is now the headquarters of the Order of the Phoenix. As you enter the London Waterfront area, look to the row of brown brick buildings to the right and find number 12. Stand back and look up at the second floor window for a glimpse of

Kreacher, the Black family house elf who is obviously irritated by all of the muggles milling around.

While in London, wander over to the red phone booth which represents the visitor entrance to the Ministry of Magic. Step inside the booth and dial the word, "Magic," to be connected to the Ministry of Magic (although due to a mischievous charm, it doesn't always work).

After returning to Hogwarts on the Hogwarts Express, Harry sees a strange creature, called a Thestral pulling the students carriages. Although you may not see the thestral, its carriage is located where the motorbike begins on the track on Hagrid's ride and listen because he mentions the beasts.

After returning to Hogwarts Castle, Harry Potter forms Dumbledore's Army, from a group of Hogwarts students. Their first meeting is at the **Hogs Head Pub.** This pub is adjacent to the Three Broomsticks is Hogsmeade. Head over there now for a Butterbeer, Pumpkin Juice or Hagrid's drink, Fire Whiskey.

Harry has a vision that Voldemort's snake, Nagini is attacking Arthur Weasley. Head to Diagon Alley. The large boa constrictor can be seen in the side window and from inside Magical Menagerie in Diagon Alley.

Harry and Dumbledore's Army travel to the Ministry of Magic and battle the Death Eaters and Bellatrix Lestrange. Death Eaters apparel can be found in Borgin and Burkes in Knockturn Alley and Bellatrix is seen on the ride, Harry Potter and the Escape from Gringotts.

Dark Magic and Wizard Wheezes

Harry's sixth year at Hogwarts is recounted in the book,

Harry Potter and the Half Blood Prince. Professor Dumbledore meets Harry near Platform 3 next to a billboard advertising Divine Magic Perfume. Enter King's Cross Station and walk along the queue until you see the billboard.

Harry and friends visit **Weasley's Wizard Wheezes** in Diagon Alley. This is the fantastically successful whimsical joke shop of which Fred and George Weasley are the proprietors. One would have to admit that this is the most iconic spot in Diagon Alley, second only to Gringotts Bank.

Wink: *Leave it to the Weasley brothers to mock Dolores Umbridge! In Weasleys Wizard Wheezes, look up while at to see the Dolores Umbridge riding a unicycle on a tight rope.*

Wizard Trivia Question No. 19: What is Weasleys Wizard Wheezes address?

While shopping for school supplies in Diagon Alley, Ron, Hermione and Harry follow Draco Malfoy to Knockturn Alley and watch through a window as Draco and Death Eaters examine a mysterious cabinet. You can find the cabinet at Borgin and Burkes in Knockturn Alley.

Wizard Trivia Question No. 20: What is the name of the vampire who attends Professor Slughorn's party.

On the way back from a snowy visit to Hogsmeade, fellow Hogwarts student, Katie Bell, is cursed by an opal necklace which was meant for Dumbledore. Return to Diagon Alley if you want to see the cursed necklace at Borgin and Burkes in Knockturn Alley.

The Dragon Escapes

The seventh book in J. K. Rowling's series, *Harry Potter and the Deathly Hallows*, starts out with Voldemort's banquet at Malfoy Manor. This location is not really on Harry's journey, but you do get a glimpse of its sinister setting on the **Hogwarts Express** train ride. Nagini, Voldemort's snake, is also at this dinner. The snake can be found in the side window at **Magical Menagerie** in Diagon Alley.

When Harry leaves the Dursleys' house for the last time, it is with a crew of decoy Harry's who have all had the aid of Polyjuice Potion. The real Harry rides in the sidecar of Hagrid's enchanted motorbike. The motorbike is found in two locations. One is parked next to Gringotts Bank in Diagon Alley (which is great for photos) and also on Hagrid's Magical Motorbike Adventure in Hogsmeade.

Wizard Trivia Question No. 21: Who is Tonks cousin?

While Harry, Ron and Hermione are in hiding, they realize that they must visit the Lovegood home. This is where Harry learns the story of the Deathly Hallows in *The Tale of the Three Brothers*, from the book, *Tales of Beedle the Bard*. In the Carkitt Market section of Diagon Alley, watch the puppet show of the same name.

Harry, Ron and Hermione are captured and taken to Malfoy Manor. They are rescued by Dobby the House Elf. There is a statue of Dobby high up on a wall near Carkitt Market in Diagon Alley between Owl Post and Sugarplums.

Wizard trivia question No. 22: For what purpose is Essence of Dittany used?

During Harry's search for horcruxes, Harry, Ron and Hermione decide to break into Bellatrix Lestrange's vault at Gringotts to steal a horcrux. Head to Gringotts bank, the most iconic landmark in Diagon Alley. Enter the ride, **Harry Potter and the Escape from Gringotts** where you encounter Harry, Ron and Hermione's on their quest to find a horcrux and encounter the dragon on which they escape. The dragon sits atop Gringotts Bank and breathes fire!

Wizard Trivia Quest No. 23: What is Dolores Umbridge's middle name?

Harry's journey through J. K. Rowling's books culminates at Hogwarts Castle with the Battle of Hogwarts. Several years later, Harry, Jenny, Ron and Hermione meet again at Platform 9 ¾ to send their children off for their own journey to Hogwarts Castle. Therefore, your journey may end at Kings Cross Station at Platform ¾.

Wizard Trivia Question No. 24: What stones are encrusted in the Sword of Gryffindor?

*"Yeah, we'll call you," muttered Ron as the knight
disappeared, "if we ever need someone mental."*
Ron Weasley
Harry Potter and the Prisoner of Azkaban

CHAPTER 9: CELEBRATIONS, CHARACTERS AND WINKS

Wizards and witches love celebrations as much as any muggle. It is no different at the Wizarding World of Harry Potter. The wizarding world has its own Christmas celebration with decorations and Christmas entertainment.

Christmas in the Wizarding World of Harry Potter

Christmas in The Wizarding World of Harry Potter is an annual event which brings the magic of Christmas to life in the wizarding world. Christmas was always a special time of year for Harry Potter in the books and films and the season is celebrated in several ways at Universal Orlando. The celebration features holiday decorations, twinkly lights, special holiday treats, drinks, and shows.

Each storefront and building in Hogsmeade, the London Waterfront and Diagon Alley is festooned with different holiday garlands. Pay special attention to these garlands as each garland sports a different theme according to where it is placed.

Christmas music is found in all three areas as well. At the London Waterfront, buskers at Kings Cross Station perform holiday tunes. On the Hogsmeade stage, themed daily holiday shows are performed multiple times a day by the Frog Choir. And in Diagon Alley, the singing sorceress, Celestina Warbeck and her Banshees perform holiday tunes every 45 minutes.

The centerpiece of the Christmas celebration in the wizarding world is the nightly Christmas themed light show which is projected on Hogwarts Castle. This spectacular show is synced with Christmas music and combined with fireworks.

Wink: *Order a hot ButterBeer to sip while watching the nightly light show at Hogwarts Castle!*

The "Uncelebration" of the Wizarding World of Harry Potter

There is a "secret" annual event that is gaining in popularity. Members of the private Facebook group, Weasleys Whimsical World of Harry Potter, missed the defunct annual Celebration of Harry Potter which previously occurred on the last weekend of January every year. They missed the event so much they created a Facebook event called, Weasley's Annual UnCelebration. The sixth annual 2024 event takes place on January 26 through 29. In past events, members of the group attended in very authentic Harry Potter character inspired costumes or cosplay. Over the days of the event, group members participate in scavenger hunts, trivia, dinners and lots and lots of photographs. There's even a kids cosplay contest with prizes! To learn more about this event, join the Facebook group, and watch Youtube videos.

Orlando Informer's Private Events

Followers of website, blog and social media of the Orlando Informer look forward each year to scheduled events which are called "Meet Ups" at Universal Orlando. These private and separately ticketed events are a fantastic way to tour the wizarding world without the larger everyday crowds! What started out as a once a year after hours event in Diagon Alley has expanded to events encompassing Universal Studios and Islands of Adventure several times per year.

The festivities begin after both parks close to the general public. The events include unlimited non-alcoholic beverages including Butterbeer as well as food and even ice cream from Florean Fortescue's Ice Cream Parlour! Only a limited number of tickets are sold at these private events to keep the lines short and less crowded.

For information on future Meet Ups, the best source of information is the Orlando Informer Facebook page, and their Facebook group. You can also register to receive emails at www.orlandoinformer.com.

Secrets and Winks

Muggles are familiar with the saying, "stop and smell the roses," but at Universal Orlando it is *Watch for Winks.* The House Elves at Universal Orlando have added little hidden details which some muggles refer to as "Easter Eggs" or "Hidden Mickeys" (a Walt Disney World phenomenon). Since Winky, the House Elf, hid most of them at Universal Orlando, we refer to them as *Winks (*you will remember Winky from the book, *Harry Potter and the Goblet of Fire*).

At the Wizarding World of Harry Potter, some of these winks are nods to past attractions. In this book, we won't give them all away as there is great joy in discovering them on your own, but here are a few hidden (or not so hidden) details which are not so obvious unless you are looking for them.

Spoiler Alert: if you would like to discover these Winks on your own, read no further!

Hogsmeade Winks

Since the Village of Hogsmeade is a little older, having opened in 2010, most of the older *Winks* have been discovered by muggles, but with the opening of Hagrid's Magical Motorbike Adventure, there came an opportunity to discover many new winks!

At Hagrid's attraction, check out these winks:

• On the entrance arch, there is a lion which is a symbol of

Hagrid's Hogwarts house, Gryffindor.

- In the outdoor queue, nestled in the trees and shrubbery is a child's wooden hippogriff.

Pay close attention to the graffiti on the walls of the ruins in the queue for quite a few winks:

- There is a hippogriff painted in graffiti when you enter the ruins. Be sure to read what is written below.

- Near the hippogriff graffiti is a heart with the initials J+L. These are the initials of Harry's parents, James and Lily.

- Near the heart are the words, "I miss my owl" written by Harry referring to Hedwig.

- Above the heart, is written, "Wit beyond measure is man's greatest treasure" which is the Ravenclaw motto and the phrase engraved on the famous diadem.

- On the wall on the left are two graffiti dragons—one blue and one red with the words Dueling Club. This is a nod to two roller coasters which held this spot previously— Dueling Dragons, the original park ride, and Dragon Challenge, the name the ride was re-themed for the wizarding world after Hogsmeade opened to the public. The dragon coasters were torn down to build Hagrid's ride.

- To the left of a door, high up on the wall is written, H & O with a heart between. These are referring to the romance of Hagrid and Madame Olympe Maxime, the headmistress of Beauxbatons Academy of Magic.

- One very overlooked wink is in the egg room. As you enter, turn around and notice the words, "Celestina is Brilliant" which was written by Molly Weasley during her school days.

As the queue continues, here are more winks:

- There are salamander footprints in the fireplace.

- The Triwizard Tournament's golden dragon egg is hidden in a green cabinet in the egg hatchery.

- In the room where Hagrid does experiments, there is a *Monster Book of Monsters* textbook on the table.

- There are animal crates which served as playpens for baby blast-ended skrewts and baby dragons. If you look closely, you'll see a teddy bear in one, placed there by Hagrid.

- There is a poster on the wall of a baby niffler, which was probably torn out of the textbook, *Care of Magical Creatures* written by Newt Scamander.

- Thestrals, magical creatures which are part bat, part horse, are mentioned by Hagrid at the beginning of the motorbike ride and a carriage that thestrals pull is on the left side of the track.

- The large blast-ended skrewt is in itself a *Wink* because it was only mentioned in the books and not included in the films. Many Muggles who have not read the stories wonder what this strange creature is.

- Devil's Snare which trapped Harry, Ron and Hermione in the first book traps riders on Hagrid's Magical Motorbike Adventure (right before a drop).

More Winks in the Village of Hogsmeade:

- In the portrait gallery in Hogwarts Castle, the four founders of Hogwarts Academy are shown with their personal belongings, some of which later become Voldemort's Horcruxes.

- The actor who portrays Gilderoy Lockhart also portrays Godric Gryffindor in his talking portrait.

- Inside the Public Conveniences (which Americans refer to as restrooms), listen for Moaning Myrtle.

- There is a howler in the window at Owl Post.

- While not so "hidden," look up at the clock tower. Instead of the normal clock chimes, an owl "hoots" at every quarter hour.

- While sitting in the covered bench area near the Owl Post, look up to see several animatronic owls. Luckily their droppings are only for show.

- Hermione's Yule Ball gown is seen in the second story window at Gladrags Wizardwear in Hogsmeade.

- Next door to Honeydukes is Zonko's Joke Shop which was the Weasley Brothers inspiration for their store. The store was open but closed with the addition of Diagon Alley.

- The sign for the Three Broomsticks represents the symbol of the Deathly Hallows.

Winks at the London Waterfront

- Kreacher often peeks out of the window at 12 Grimmauld

Place, the home of Sirius Black.

• At Kings Cross Station, as you head to Platform 9 ¾, there are several winks to notice. Upon entering, notice the "London" chill in the air.

• The Divine Magic billboard appeared in *Harry Potter and the Half Blood Prince*.

• In the Record Shop window, notice the record, Joe Sez No. This refers to J. K. Rowling's creative control of the wizarding world. The author said "no" to many creative ideas during the planning of the area.

• At the Grimmauld Place row of houses, all house numbers are odd numbers with the exception of number 12, the Black family house.

• Don't be in such a hurry that you miss reading the advertisements when walking through the queue in Kings Cross Station. The best one is the Divine Magic perfume billboard reminiscent of the one in front of which Dumbledore appeared to Harry in the film *Harry Potter and the Half Blood Prince*.

• On Platform 9 ¾, look for Hedwig's cage on a student trolley.

Winks at Diagon Alley

When Diagon Alley opened in 2014, muggles were amazed at the fire breathing dragon, wizard shops, and casting spells. It takes a few visits to this area to notice all of the *Winks* that were placed there. Most muggles discover something new on each visit. It would ruin the fun of discovery to name them all so here are a few:

• At Magical Menagerie, a shop full of plush animals found

within the books and films, notice the alley to the left of the store. In the window is Nagini, the large pet snake and Horcrux of "He Who Must Not Be Named."

- While you are looking at the snake in the window at Magical Menagerie from inside the shop, look closely to notice that there is another snake. This is the snake that Harry set free from the zoo in the first book.

- For another Wink at Magical Menagerie, look up to see Luna Lovegood's favorite creature which other wizards don't believe exists, the Triple-Horned Snorkack, and several other magical creatures on the second level.

- The sign outside the Leaky Cauldron actually leaks (inside of Diagon Alley).

- In the window at Spindlewarps, see the same knitting needles which are seen at Molly Weasley's house.

- Notice the magical beasts flanking the top points of Eternelle's Elixir of Life. You can see a unicorn, hippogriff, thestral, Dementor and more.

- Next to Gringotts Bank is a golden statue of a goblin standing on stacked gold galleons. This is the goblin, Gringott.

- A Monster Book of Monsters is on display in Flourish & Blotts shop window as well as books by Gilderoy Lockhart. Read the names of the stacked books.

Knockturn Alley Winks

- At Borgin and Burkes, there are several *Winks* to discover. Several of Voldemort's Horcruxes are displayed including the Ravenclaw's diadem, Marvolo's ring and Hufflepuff's cup.

- The cursed necklace from the film, *Harry Potter and the Half Blood Prince*, is in a glass case.

- The Hand of Glory which grabbed Harry in the film, *Harry Potter and the Chamber of Secrets* is in a glass case in Borgen and Burkes.

- A bird can be heard singing in Draco's vanishing cabinet from the film, *Harry Potter and the Half Blood Prince.*

- A Bogart is trapped in a chest from the film, *Harry Potter and the Prisoner of Azkaban.* This is located under a table in Borgin and Burkes.

- Try turning the all of door knobs in Knockturn Alley and you may get a surprise.

Remembering Jaws

Many muggles were in quite a snit upon learning that their beloved original park attraction, Jaws, was going to be replaced by Diagon Alley. In respect for the memory of Jaws, not only has the giant great white hanging shark, affectionately named "Bruce," been moved to the San Francisco area in Universal Studios (with a view of the London Waterfront), but a few *Winks* have also been placed in Diagon Alley.

- In the window of the Record shop on the London waterfront is a record titled *Here's to Swimming' with Bowlegged Women* by the Quint Trio which was mentioned by Quint in the Jaws film. The Quint Trio refers to the three main characters' names.

- Telescopes and brass pieces inside Wiseacre's Gift Shop are made with pieces of old boats and from the queue of the Jaws ride.

- A shark's jaw is seen inside the window of the Apothecary shop and also in Borgin and Burkes.

- A group of singing shrunken heads in Knockturn Alley occasionally sing a familiar tune, *Show Me the Way to Go Home*, which was drunkenly sung by the characters in the film, *Jaws*.

Characters Greetings at the Wizarding World

One reason that Ms. Rolling approved the creation of the Wizarding World of Harry Potter at Universal Orlando instead of Walt Disney World was that she was adamant that there would be no characters greetings. For this reason, you will never get a picture with Harry, Ron, Hermione, Dumbledore or Professor Snape. However, there are "characters" with which to meet and possibly take photos.

In Hogsmeade:

Meet the Hogwarts Express conductor in front of the train engine just outside of Hogsmeade Station.

Members of the Frog Choir are available for photos for a few minutes after performances.

The students of Beauxbatons Academy and Durmstrang Academy are available for photos for a few minutes after performances.

The snowman in Hogsmeade is available year round for your photos (due to a charm to prevent him from melting).

At the London Waterfront:

Meet the Knight Bus conductor and talking shrunken head at the Knight Bus.

At Diagon Alley:

Meet the Goblin clerk at Gringotts Money Exchange. You will also see many goblins in the queue at Harry Potter and the Escape from Gringotts.

"I'm Not Wearing That, It's Ghastly."
Ginny Weasley
Harry Potter and the Goblet of Fire

CHAPTER 10: AN OWL, A SNITCH, AND A WIZARD'S ROBE

O f all of the attractions in the Wizarding World of Harry Potter at Universal Orlando, shopping for magical souvenirs may be the most popular—even more popular than Hagrid's ride! Diagon Alley is the best area overall for the sheer number of shops and various souvenirs available for purchase.

Best Wizarding World Souvenirs

What each Harry Potter fan considers as the best souvenir greatly varies from muggle to muggle. There are as many choices of souvenirs as there are magical beasts is the forbidden forest! Souvenirs can be grouped by your favorite

Hogwarts House and muggles can purchase anything from bags and gloves to temporary tattoos and even beach towels! Some of the most popular souvenirs are listed here for you. We will start with...a wand!

Wink: *To get an idea of what types of souvenirs are offered, go to UniversalOrlando.com and click the "Shop Merchandise" link. There is an entire Harry Potter section.*

No. 1 Souvenir: The Interactive Wand

A wand is a fantastic choice for a souvenir because not only is it a collectible souvenir, but also a tool for the interactive wand experiences in both theme parks. Purchasing a wand by attending Ollivanders "Wand Chooses the Wizard" ceremony is a rite of passage for new visiting muggles to the wizarding world. The map enclosed may also look nice framed as wall art for your personal Potter collection.

While all wands from the wizarding world are considered collectible, there is one major difference—interactive or non-interactive. Before the opening of Diagon Alley, only non-interactive wands were offered for purchase. After Diagon Alley opened, interactive wands took over as the best sellers. These "magical" wands allow muggles to cast spells in shop windows with magical effects. The average price for an interactive wand is $63 US dollars while non-interactive sell for about $55. Believe it or not, Mr. Ollivander is still creating new wands and several new styles recently went on sale in all of the stores where wands are offered and online. Muggles may also purchase character wands from well known witches and wizards from the books—Voldemort, Harry, Hermione, Luna, Ron, Jenny and even Hagrid's disguised umbrella wand!

Wink: *If you wish to take your time while shopping for a wand, Ollivanders may not be the best place to slowly look* *at all of the wands available due to the crowds and limited space. A great place to shop for wands is the Universal store in CityWalk. There is a large Harry Potter section with great wand displays.*

Note: According to the website, collectible wands are fragile and not meant to be toys.

No. 2 Souvenir: House Robes

True Harry Potter geeks need Hogwarts Academy house robes. These robes are made of lightweight, breathable fabric which is necessary when wearing in Florida. The robes have the house insignias of the four Hogwarts houses and and inside wand pocket.

No. 3 Souvenir: Marauders Map

The Marauders Map is a true bit of muggle magic. These maps show the footsteps of several characters including Snape. The map comes with a special wand whose magic only works on the map.

No. 4 Souvenir: Chocolate Frog Cards

You can imagine why Harry Potter geeks love these souvenirs. It's something that magical folks also collect! Each chocolate frog box comes with a collectible card.

Other Great Souvenirs

What makes a great souvenir differs between guests but in my opinion, the best souvenir is something you will use regularly. Here are some good choices:

- Apparel—T-shirts, sweatshirts, jackets, scarves, Quidditch jerseys, etc.
- Lanyards (useful for your park admission passes while touring the parks)
- Coffee tumblers
- Purses and backpacks
- Key chains
- Jewelry
- Toys and Plushes—Hedwig is a most popular plush toy and puppet!
- Dinnerware

Here are a couple of "out of the box" souvenirs:

- Send yourself a postcard or letter with wizarding world stamps from Owl Post with a Hogsmeade postmark!

- Send your purchased souvenirs in Owl Post brown paper packaging—just like how Hogwarts students receive them in the great hall!

- Wizarding world Pressed Penny collectibles are available in pressed penny machines in the Harry Potter section in Universal Stores at the theme parks.

Wink: *Many muggles shop in advance of visiting the wizarding world so that they have apparel to wear to the theme parks. Shopping online may also be a better choice for heavier items which can be inconvenient for air travel. Interactive wands are sometimes found at online sites like Ebay.com.*

Listed below are the shops in each area of the wizarding world.

FYI: Besides the wizarding world shops, magical merchandise, apparel and interactive wands can be found in other areas:

Universal CityWalk: Universal Store
Onsite Resort Gift Shops
Universal's Islands of Adventure: Sahara Traders in Port of
Entry
Universal Studios: Universal Store at the Entrance in
Production Central

And...if you forgot something, there is a large Universal Store
with lots of Harry Potter merchandise in the Orlando
International Airport.

The London Waterfront Shop

London Taxi Hut

At the London Waterfront, the London Taxi Hut across
from Kings Cross Station is the only shopping to be found in
this area. Although it is a small outdoor stand, it is the best
place to buy Knight Bus souvenirs, figurines and t-shirts and
also sells Hogwarts Express merchandise.

The Shops of Diagon Alley

Ollivanders Wand Shop

Ollivanders is the best place of choice for the experience
of purchasing a wand, but there are other items for sale as
well in this shop. The clerks will also magically "repair"
interactive wands in this shop.

Weasleys Wizard Wheezes

This is perhaps the most iconic shop in Diagon Alley!
The bright orange store front foretells of the whimsically
mischievous merchandise found within. This emporium will

equip a fledgling charms caster with all manner of mischief such as magical jokes, tricks, and toys including Pygmy Puffs, U-No-Poo pills, Skiving Snackboxes, Puking Pastilles, and more. A muggle favorite is the Dolores Umbridge toy riding a unicycle which can be seen from above in the shop.

Wizard Trivia Question No. 25: What was Dolores Umbridge's title at the Ministry of Magic before becoming the Defense Against the Dark Arts teacher at Hogwarts?

Gringotts Money Exchange

The main appeal of this spot is to exchange muggle currency for Wizarding World money but also to speak to the grumpy goblin clerk and take selfies. There are a few Gringotts themed items for sale as well as gold wrapped chocolate galleon coins.

Madam Malkin's Robes for all Occasions

This is a great place to purchase Hogwarts house robes, sweaters, ties, socks, lanyards and more. Stand in front of the mirror for comments on your outfit!

Globus Mundi

This magical travel agency equips travelers with Hogwarts Express themed goods as well as themed Globus Mundi merchandise. This shop may be closed on low attendance days.

Magical Menagerie

This shop is where you can purchase all your favorite magical beasts. Hedwig, Pigwidgeon, Crookshanks, toads, and a varied supply of fantastical beast plushes are sold in this shop.

Quality Quidditch Supplies

Golden Snitches, bludgers, brooms and all types of Quidditch supplies and apparel are for sale in this sporty shop.

Scribbulus

This shop is a writer's paradise! Inside these walls, you can find writing implements, journals, backpacks and more. The window outside is a popular spot for casting spells with interactive wands.

Sugarplum's Sweet Shop

Like Honeydukes in Hogsmeade, Sugarplum's has all of the wizarding world sweets as well as baked goods such as Cauldron Cakes, Butterbeer fudge and Pumpkin Pasties.

Wands by Gregorovitch

Proprietor Mykew Gregorovitch is Mr. Ollivander's biggest competitor in the wand game. This outdoor wand stand is popular with those of Slytherin House. This shop is often closed on low attendance days.

Wiseacre's Wizarding Equipment

Guests exit Harry Potter and the Escape from Gringotts through this shop which carries a varied supply of souvenirs including apparel, figurines, ornaments and more.

The Knockturn Alley Shop

The one and only shop found in Knockturn Alley carries some of the most popular dark goods which are especially popular with those of the Slytherin house.

Borgin and Burkes

This creepy shop has not only great merchandise for sale but also some dark artifacts to see including Draco's vanishing cabinet, the Hand of Glory, the Cursed Necklace, the diadem and a Bogart trapped in a trunk. Among the dimly lit shelves, you'll find items for sale such as Death Eater masks, skulls, costume replicas from the films, apparel, accessories, jewelry, and collectibles.

The Shops of Hogsmeade

The Village of Hogsmeade, the original section of the wizarding world has quite a few shops to peruse for magical merchandise. Universal sometimes changes around merchandise, but these are what was on offer at the time of publication.

Ollivanders Wand Shop

The original Ollivanders shop has all of the wands you could want to choose. Most muggles enter the shop after attending the Wand Chooses the Wizard Show. The person chosen at the show has the option to buy the wand selected or choose their own to purchase. Wands are sold individually but there are also collectible sets.

Honeydukes

The bright pink and green interior will brighten even the darkest wizard's mood. Honeydukes carries a varied array of sweets including chocolate frogs, peppermint toads, licorice wands and assorted sweets sold by weight. There is also a bakery case with candy apples fudge and the most popular item, Cauldron Cakes.

Dervish and Banges

Here you can find Hogwarts house jerseys and merchandise as well as Quidditch supplies. At this shop, you may also purchase replicas of the Goblet of Fire and the TriWizard Cup.

Filch's Emporium of Confiscated Goods

Mr. Filch has a varied collection of Hogwarts Academy and Hogwarts Express merchandise but the most valued item may be the interactive Maurauders' Map. There is also quite a selection of Christmas ornaments for sale year round.

Owl Post

At Owl Post, you can purchase not only wands and assorted wizard gear, but you may also purchase stationary, buy themed stamps and send letters and packages with an authentic Hogsmeade postmark through the U.S. mail.

FYI: For more information on merchandise available, visit UniversalOrlando.com and tap Shop Merchandise and then tap Harry Potter to view an array of items for sale.

"Percy wouldn't recognize a joke if it danced naked in front of him wearing Dobby's tea cozy."
Ron Weasley
Harry Potter and the Goblet of Fire

CHAPTER 11: FANTASTIC EATS AND WHERE TO FIND THEM

xperiencing the magic of the Wizarding World of Harry Potter is an exhilarating experience, but can also be exhausting and can make wizards and muggles quite hungry and thirsty. Luckily, at the wizarding world, there is a great variety of meals, snacks, treats and drinks.

When building The Wizarding World of Harry Potter at Universal Orlando that clever British witch, J. K. Rowling, insisted on a distinctly British influence when replicating areas of London and Scotland. There is no sign of any American products anywhere to be found in these area. If you want American brands of soda or merchandise, you must exit the Wizarding World and visit other areas. Which means, if you have a Coke Freestyle refillable cup, refill it before entering.

There are three areas in the Wizarding World of Harry Potter in which to find refreshments: Hogsmeade, Diagon Alley and the London Waterfront.

Wizard Trivia Question No. 26: At what location was Harry when he first learned that Sirius Black was his Godfather?

Magical Beverages

This may be a chapter about "fantastic eats," but "fantastic drinks" must also be mentioned! The heat of the Florida can cause a mighty thirst whether you are a witch, wizard, or muggle. While Butterbeer has gained the greatest popularity, there are several magical concoctions for quenching the thirsty palate. These beverages can be found at several locations in both Diagon Alley and Hogsmeade.

Butterbeer

In *Harry Potter and the Prisoner of Azkaban*, Harry developed his love of Butterbeer. This foamy brew truly tastes of the magic of the wizarding world with hints of butterscotch, caramel, cream soda with a layer of whipped cream atop its sugary and fizzy sweetness. The frozen variety has the same butterscotch flavored goodness in a slushy frozen concoction. For a short time during the year when the weather turns cooler, don't miss trying out Hot Butterbeer when it is offered. Butterbeer is served in a plastic cup or in a souvenir mug.

Wink: *There are seven different ways to enjoy the Butterbeer flavour.*

Original Butterbeer
Frozen Butterbeer
Hot Butterbeer
Butterbeer soft serve ice cream (at Florean Fortescue's)
Butterbeer hard-packed ice cream (at Three Broomsticks)
Butterbeer fudge (at Sugarplum's)
Butterbeer Potted Cream (at Leaky Cauldron)

Pumpkin Juice

Pumpkin Juice may have been the first beverage Harry was served when he arrived at Hogwarts Castle for the first time at the great feast in *Harry Potter and the Sorcerer's Stone*. The pumpkin flavored drink has touches of winter spices such as cinnamon and cloves. Pumpkin juice is available on tap at the Fountain of Fair Fortune, Hopping Pot, Hogs Head Pub and at the Three Broomsticks. A carbonated version, Pumpkin Fizz is also available at the Three Broomsticks.

Tongue Tying Lemon Squash

Sometimes, the simplicity of lemonade is magical and refreshing. This very tart lemonade drink with a hint of vanilla is served over ice with the addition of added fresh-squashed lemon, which adds just enough citrus to temporarily "tie the tongue." This drink is sold at all beverage locations in Diagon Alley.

Peachtree Fizzing Tea

What could be more refreshing in the Florida heat than this peach flavored, slightly fizzy iced tea? The light peach flavour with a hint of ginger slightly sweetens the tea and is a great alternative to some of the other overly sweet beverages offered in the wizarding world. This drink is sold at all beverage locations in Diagon Alley.

Fishy Green Ale

This is probably the most fun drink of all. It is a cloudy and slightly creamy light green drink with a hint of carbonation. The tall cup has a minty flavour and a hint of cinnamon. The drink is finished with a handful of blueberry popping pearls for an extra burst of flavor. This drink is sold at all beverage locations in Diagon Alley.

Otter's Fizzy Orange Juice

Fred and George Weasley invented this fun fizzy orange drink which was originally sold at Weasley Wizard Wheezes. A favorite of Diagon Alley, it has hint of vanilla and an orange slice. This drink is sold at all locations in Diagon Alley.

Witches and Wizards Brews

There are two exclusive beer brews created in Florida for Diagon Alley. These specialty brews are craft beers, magically brewed and bursting with flavour. These are available for around $10 and served in a tall cup.

Dragon Scale, as the name would have it, is a fiery brew and is the lighter of the two brews. While being a little strong on the malt flavour, it is the more preferred beer of Muggles. The dark **Wizard's Brew** might have had an origin in Knockturn Alley due to its porter darkness. It is the sweeter of the two beers. These two brews are available at the Leaky Cauldron, The Hopping Pot, and Fountain of Fair Fortune.

Eternelle's Elixir of Refreshment

There are four magical beverages to try at Eternelle's and muggles can blend them. This forbidding kiosk in Diagon Alley is flanked on every corner by magical beasts. The offerings here are magical elixirs to mix into Gilly Water (bottled water). Each elixir comes in a vial which makes a nice souvenir. Elixirs and Gilly Water are about $4 each.

Draught of Peace - Calming Berry Flavor with Blueberry, Blackberry, Raspberry, and Cherry
Babbling Beverage - Whimsical Mouthwatering Fruit Punch
Fire Protection Potion - Cooling Watermelon Flavor with Peach and Strawberry Tones
Elixir to Induce Euphoria - Happy Pineapple flavor with hints of Green Apple and Mint

The London Waterfront Eats

Outside of Diagon Alley in the London Waterfront area, there are two London Taxi Huts which offer merchandise for sale and British street fare.

London Taxi Hut

Cab shelters, also known as taxi huts are a familiar site in London. These were constructed in Victorian times to provide low cost meals and shelter for London hackney cab drivers.

In more recent times, these shelters have been converted for the purpose of selling wares and snacks. At Universal, the London Taxi Hut menu provides some of Britain's favorite street fare, jacket potatoes (commonly known in America as baked potatoes) with a variety of toppings which makes them a hearty meal. Also available is a theme park staple, the hot dog, encased in a roll which is magically toasted on the inside, and crisps (known as potato chips in the United States).

Menu
Hot Dog with Crisps $13.99

Jacket Potato with beans and cheese $10.49
Jacket Potato with broccoli and cheese $10.49
Shepherd's Pie Jacket Potato $10.49
Loaded Jacket Potato $10.49

Crisps $3.50

Drinks:
Bottled Tea $4.79
Bottled Juice $4.79
Bottled Water $5.00
Canned Beer $9.00

Dining in Diagon Alley

When Harry entered the world of magic, one of the best surprises was the fantastic food! After living with the Dursley's for 10 years and sometimes practically starved, the wonderful meals were literally the cherry on top of the pudding!

At Diagon Alley, there are more authentic examples of British fare than in Hogsmeade.

The Leaky Cauldron

Hagrid's favorite spot, The Leaky Cauldron, is open to hungry Muggles from all over the world. It is a combination of witchy decor and satisfying meals. Breakfast, lunch and dinner are served at this fine establishment which feature staples of British fare.

Leaky Cauldron Menus

Breakfast - served until 10:30 am daily
Includes small beverage

Traditional Breakfast - $17.99
Fresh scrambled eggs, sausage links, black pudding, English bacon, baked beans, grilled tomato, sautéed mushrooms and breakfast potatoes

Pancake Breakfast - $17.99
Three fluffy buttermilk pancakes, crisp bacon and link sausage with butter croissant

American Breakfast - $17.99
Fresh scrambled eggs, breakfast potatoes, crisp bacon, and link sausage with butter croissant

Apple Oatmeal Flan with Yogurt & Fruit - $17.99
Freshly baked flan of apples and oatmeal served with yogurt and fresh seasonal fruit

Egg, Leek, & Mushroom Pasty - $17.99
Pastry wrapped scrambled eggs, mushrooms and leeks served with breakfast potatoes and fresh fruit

Kid's Breakfast - $12.99
Choose traditional, pancake or American

Sides

Bacon - $2.19
Blood Sausage - $5.49
English Bacon - $4.99
Scrambled Eggs - $2.49
Roasted Potatoes - $4.49

Beverages

Pumpkin Juice™ - $4.99
Hot Tea - $3.49
Fresh Brewed Coffee - $3.49
Milk - $2.49
Apple Juice - $2.99
Orange Juice - $2.99

Tip: Choose Butterbeer in your favorite version as your included beverage.

Lunch And Dinner Menu:

Entrées

Fish & Chips - $16.99
Fresh north Atlantic cod battered and fried with chips and tartar sauce

Bangers & Mash - $14.49
Roasted English sausage, creamy mashed potatoes, roasted tomatoes, sautéed onions and cabbage, minted peas & onion gravy

Toad in the Hole - $12.49
A popular dish of English sausage baked into a Yorkshire pudding and served with onion gravy, minted peas, root vegetables and roasted tomato

Beef, Lamb & Guinness Stew - $16.49
Served in a warm, crusty bread bowl

Cottage Pie - $16.49
Savory combination of beef and chunky vegetables in a potato crust served with a garden salad

Fisherman's Pie - $17.49

Salmon, shrimp and cod baked together under a potato crust served with garden salad

Mini Pie Combination - $16.99
Mini cottage pie and mini fisherman's pie served with garden salad

Scotch Eggs - $11.49
Served warm with apple beet salad and mustard sauce

Soup & Salad - $11.99
Split pea and ham soup served with side garden salad

Irish Stew - $16.49
Vegan beef tip and potato stew; served with vegan crusty bread and side garden salad

Shepherd's Pasty Pie - $16.49
Meatless beef crumbles and vegetable stew hand pie; served with creamy stone ground mustard dipping sauce, apple beet salad, and wedge fries

Ploughman's - $21.99. Serves 2
A feast of English cheese, crusty bread, field green salad, roasted tomatoes, cornichon pickles, apple beet salad, Branston pickle & scotch eggs

Sides

Wedge Fries - $4.49
Scotch Egg - $4.99
Mashed Potatoes with Gravy - $3.49
Add Banger (1 each) - $4.99
Side Garden Salad - $6.99

Sandwiches
Served with wedge fries. Gluten-free buns are available upon request.

Banger - $12.99
Roasted English sausage, mustard aioli, roasted tomatoes, sautéed cabbage and onions on a crusted baguette

Specialty Chicken - $14.49
Grilled chicken breast, apple butter mayo, Colby cheese, smoky apple bacon, roasted tomatoes on a housemade specialty bun

Kids' Entrées

Macaroni Cheese - $7.49
served with grapes and applesauce

Fish & Chips - $7.49
served with chips and tartar sauce

Mini Pie - $7.49
served with grapes and applesauce

Desserts
All bakery items are made in a facility where cross-contamination with gluten, soy, peanuts, and tree nuts is possible.

Sticky Toffee Pudding - $7.49
Cranachan - $6.99
Butterbeer™ Potted Cream - $5.99
Chocolate Potted Cream - $4.99
Butterbeer™ Ice Cream - $5.99
Cup of Ice Cream - $5.99
Strawberry and Peanut Butter, Vanilla or Chocolate

Beverages

Butterbeer™ - $7.99
A non-alcoholic sweet drink reminiscent of shortbread and

butterscotch

Frozen Butterbeer™ - $7.99
A non-alcoholic sweet drink reminiscent of shortbread and butterscotch

Hot Butterbeer™ - $7.99
A non-alcoholic sweet drink reminiscent of shortbread and butterscotch

Pumpkin Juice™ - $4.99

Tongue Tying Lemon Squash - $5.49
Sweet and tart lemon flavored beverage served with squashed lemon

Otter's Fizzy Orange Juice - $5.49
Effervescent fresh orange beverage with notes of vanilla and cinnamon

Fishy Green Ale - $5.49
Smooth and creamy with notes of mint and cinnamon and popping blueberry fish eggs

Peachtree Fizzing Tea - $5.49
Fizzy but smooth with flavors of fresh peach nectar and ginger

Fountain Beverages - $4.29—Iced Tea, Lemonade, Cider
Gillywater - $5.50
Hot Beverages - $3.49
Coffee, Decaf, Hot Tea—2% Milk - $2.49
Chocolate Milk - $2.49
Juice - $2.99—orange, apple

Beer

Specialty Draught Beer - $12.00 Wizard's Brew, Dragon

Scale

Draught Beer - $10.50
Amstel Light, Heineken, Newcastle Brown Ale, Stella Artois,
Strongbow, Yuengling

Wine by the Glass - $9.00—Chardonnay, Cabernet
Sauvignon
Fire Whisky - $11.50

Florean Fortescue's Ice Cream Parlour

As the Florida heat intensifies, a stop in at Harry's
favorite ice cream parlour is exactly what the doctor ordered.
Florean's offers a unique array of flavours in soft serve and
hand-packed ice creams.

The showpiece flavour is the striped soft serve
Butterbeer Ice Cream. Florean Fortescue's Ice-Cream
Parlour appeared in *Harry Potter and the Prisoner of
Azkaban* when Mr. Fortescue himself gave Harry free ice
cream sundaes every half hour. Ice cream is served here in
waffle cones and plastic souvenir sundae glasses.

Flavours include hard packed ice cream and soft serve.
The soft serve has a magical element which creates a striped
effect for extra flavour. Single orders can contain two
different flavours, and you can add unusual toppings like
shortbread crumbles and meringue pieces.

Features

Butterbeer™ Ice-Cream (soft serve)
Served in a Waffle Cone - 5.99, Served in a Souvenir Glass -
8.49

Chocolate Strawberry Peanut-Butter Sundae - $10.49
Strawberry peanut-butter ice cream with hot fudge, whipped

cream and shortbread crumbles.
Served in a souvenir glass

Soft Serve Ice-Cream
Banana, Chocolate, Granny Smith, Mint, Pistachio, Vanilla, Orange Marmalade, Toffee, Toffee Apple, Strawberries & Cream
Served in a Waffle Cone - $5.99, Served in a Souvenir Glass - $8.49

Hard Pack Ice-Cream
Chocolate Chili, Apple Crumble, Vanilla, Salted Caramel Blondie, Chocolate, Clotted Cream, Earl Grey & Lavender, Sticky Toffee Pudding, Chocolate & Raspberry, Strawberry & Peanut Butter
Served in a Waffle Cone - $6.99, Served in a Souvenir Glass - $9.49

Sundaes
Served in a souvenir glass with whipped cream and a cherry

Hot Fudge Sundae - $10.49
Hot Caramel Sundae - $10.49
Strawberry Topping Sundae - $10.49

Toppings
Hundreds-and-Thousands, Shortbread Crumbles, Waffle Cone Pieces, Crystals, Chocolate Chips, Chopped Nuts - $1.19 each

Wizard Trivia Question No. 27:   What flavour ice cream did Hagrid bring to Harry on his first visit Diagon Alley?

The Hopping Pot

The Hopping Pot, named for a story from *The Tales of*

Beedle the Bard, is an outdoor pub style bar with counter service and picnic tables. This is a good place to grab a beverage and snack. Take a seat at one of the tables and enjoy a show by the magical songstress, Celestina Warbeck or one the Tales of Beedle the Bard shows.

Everyday Menu

Non-Alcoholic Drinks

Butterbeer™ - $7.99
A non-alcoholic sweet drink reminiscent of shortbread and butterscotch

Frozen Butterbeer™ - $7.99
A non-alcoholic sweet frozen drink reminiscent of shortbread and butterscotch

Hot Butterbeer™ - $7.99
A non-alcoholic sweet hot drink reminiscent of shortbread and butterscotch

Tongue Tying Lemon Squash - $5.49
Sweet and tart lemon flavored beverage served with squashed lemon

Otter's Fizzy Orange Juice - $5.49
Effervescent fresh orange beverage with notes of vanilla and cinnamon

Fishy Green Ale - $5.49
Smooth and creamy with notes of mint and cinnamon and popping blueberry fish eggs

Peachtree Fizzing Tea - $5.49
Fizzy but smooth with flavors of fresh peach nectar and ginger

Pumpkin Juice™ - $4.99
Gillywater - $5.50
Coffee - $3.49
Hot Tea - $3.49

Alcoholic Drinks

Draught Beer —Wizard's Brew, Dragon Scale, Stella Artois-
$12.00
Yuengling- $10.50
Amstel Light, Heineken, Newcastle Brown Ale, Strongbow-
$11.50
Fire Whisky - $11.50
Wine - $9.00—choice of Chardonnay or Cabernet Sauvignon

Food

Beef Pasties - $10.49
Butterbeer™ Ice Cream(ES, GS, SS)- $5.49
Chips - $3.49

Fountain of Fair Fortune

This quick service counter, named after a story in *The Tales of Beedle the Bard*, is a great stop for quick refreshment. The menu includes these beverages:

Drinks Menu

Draught Beer
Dragon Scale, Wizard's Brew - $12.00
Amstel Light, Strongbow, Yuengling - $10.50

Beverages

Butterbeer™ - $7.99
A non-alcoholic sweet drink reminiscent of shortbread and butterscotch

Frozen Butterbeer™ - $7.99
A non-alcoholic sweet drink reminiscent of shortbread and butterscotch

Pumpkin Juice™ - $4.99

Fishy Green Ale - $5.49
Smooth and creamy with notes of mint and cinnamon and popping blueberry fish eggs

Iced Tea - $4.29 Raspberry Iced Tea, Sweet Tea, Unsweetened Tea

Bottled Beverages

Gillywater - $5.50
Bottled Drinks - $4.69 Lemonade, Sweet Tea

Fire Whisky - $11.50
Fire & Strongbow Cocktail - $14.50

Food Offerings

Butterbeer™ Soft Serve Ice Cream - $5.49
Chips - $3.49

Weasley's Wizard Wheezes

The highly successful Weasley brothers began their career with their joke shop and a creative propensity for pranks disguised as sweets (much to Dudley Dursley's despair). The brothers have promised that all goods sold in Diagon Alley are safe for muggle consumption.

Popular Wheezes:

Fainting Fancies: Large round citrus flavoured gummy

candies coated in sugar.

Nosebleed Nougat: Milk chocolate covered marshmallow topped with pistachios and white candy coated chocolate balls.

Puking Pastilles: The box describes them as "hard boiled sweets," however they are diamond shaped green and purple sticky candy.

Fever Fudge: Vanilla flavoured fudge embedded with fiery jelly beans.

U-No-Poo: Green in color, these are candy coated chocolate lentils.

Skiving Snackbox: The Weasley's most famous and exclusive sweets assortment includes four types of candy: Fainting Fancies, Nosebleed Nuggets, Fever Fudge, and Puking Pastilles.

Dining in Hogsmeade

At the original location of the wizarding world, there are many flavorful delights to try.

The Butterbeer Keg

One place that adds such charm in the Village of Hogsmeade are the big red ButterBeer kegs. From these carts, cups of ButterBeer in the three varieties are available. Purchasing a Butterbeer from the big red keg has become a rite a passage for newcomers to the wizarding world.

Note: The line for the ButterBeer Kegs can become quite long early in the day. For a shorter line, perhaps you should order this beverage at the Hog's Head Pub.

ButterBeer Menu

$7.99
$13.49 souvenir mug (refill, $7.99)

Original Butterbeer
Frozen Butterbeer
Hot Butterbeer

Wink: *Straws are not offered when purchasing a traditional ButterBeer. Rumor has it that a Slytherin wizard placed a jinx on the sweet concoction. Knowing Muggles' love of straws, if you attempt to drink your Butterbeer through a straw, it tends to blow up!*

The Three Broomsticks

Harry's first taste of Butterbeer was at The Three Broomsticks in Hogsmeade Village. When you step inside this establishment, you'll feel as if you've stepped into the pages of *Harry Potter and the Prisoner of Azkaban.* This establishment is more than the average quick service theme park restaurant. The hearty menu includes American and British fare.

Muggles have a habit of visiting theme parks with large families or groups. One menu item fits the bill for a large group. The "Great Feast Platter" which is meant for 4, will easily feed a few more. It includes four full size ears of corn, roasted potatoes, fresh vegetables, ribs and roasted chicken. For a sweet treat, try the Freshly Baked Apple Pie, with raisins, fall spices and an apple crumble topping.

The Three Broomsticks Menu

Breakfast Menu
Served until 10:30 am daily
Adult 17.99 Children 12.99

Traditional English Breakfast
Fresh scrambled eggs, sausage links, black pudding, English bacon, baked beans, grilled tomato, sautéed mushrooms and breakfast potatoes.

Porridge Breakfast
Old fashioned steamed oats with fresh fruit and butter croissant.

Continental Breakfast
A colorful array of fresh fruit served with croissants accompanied with assorted jams.

Pancake Breakfast
Three fluffy buttermilk pancakes, crisp bacon, and link sausage with butter croissant.

American Breakfast
Fresh scrambled eggs, breakfast potatoes, crisp bacon, and link sausage with butter croissant.

Breakfast Beverages
Pumpkin Juice™ - $4.99
Hot Tea - $3.49
Fresh Brewed Coffee - $3.49
Juice - $2.49 Apple, Orange
Milk - $2.29 - 2%, Chocolate

The Great Feast
The Great Feast- $69.99 Platter for Four.
The first course will be a fresh garden salad tossed with our signature vinaigrette dressing. The main course will be a combination of rotisserie smoked chicken & spareribs, corn on the cob, and roast potatoes.

Additional Serving - $17.99 per person

Main Courses

Shepherd's Pie with Garden Salad- $16.49
Ground beef, lamb & vegetables crowned with potatoes

Fish and Chips- $16.99
Fresh north Atlantic cod battered & fried with chips and
tartar sauce

Beef Pasties with Garden Salad - $11.49
Flakey pastry pies filled with ground beef, vegetables &
potatoes served with a side salad & choice of dressing

Rotisserie Smoked Chicken - $14.99
Served with corn on the cob and roasted potatoes

Spareribs Platter - $18.99
Served with corn on the cob and roasted potatoes.

Chicken and Ribs Platter - $17.99
Served with corn on the cob and roasted potatoes.

Smoked Turkey Leg - $16.49
Served with wedge fries

Mushroom Pie Platter - $15.99
Stewed jackfruit and mushroom pie served with a cucumber,
tomato side salad with lemon Thyme vinaigrette dressing

Salads
Request no croutons for gluten-sensitive options

Soup & Salad Combo - $11.99
Leek & Potato or Split Pea & Ham Soup, Side salad and
choice of dressing

Rotisserie Smoked Chicken Salad - $12.49
Over a bed of fresh greens with choice of dressing (usually dark meat chicken)

Soup - $5.99 Leek & Potato or Split Pea

Beverages

Butterbeer™ is suitable for those with gluten, soy, egg, wheat and nut allergies. The topping does contain trace amounts of dairy so it is unsuitable for vegans or anyone with a dairy allergy.

Butterbeer™ - $7.99
A non-alcoholic sweet drink reminiscent of shortbread and butterscotch

Frozen Butterbeer™ - $7.99
A non-alcoholic sweet drink reminiscent of shortbread and butterscotch

Hot Butterbeer™ - $7.99
A non-alcoholic sweet drink reminiscent of shortbread and butterscotch

Pumpkin Juice™ - $4.99
Pumpkin Fizz - $4.99
Lemonade - $4.29
Cider (Non-Alcoholic) - $4.29 Apple or Pear
Iced Tea - $4.29 Sweet, Unsweetened, Raspberry, Lemonade Mix
Gillywater - $5.50
Sparkling Water - $5.50
Hot Beverages - $3.49 coffee, hot tea, hot cocoa
Milk - $2.29 choice of 2% or chocolate

Draught Beers

Draught Beer - $12.00
Hog`s Head™ Brew or Dragon Scale

Desserts

Butterbeer™ Potted Cream - $5.99
Butterbeer™ Ice Cream - $5.99
Cup of Ice Cream - $5.99, Strawberry and Peanut Butter,
Vanilla or Chocolate
Freshly Baked Apple Pie - $4.49
Chocolate Trifle - $4.99
Layered chocolate cake with fresh berries & cream

Children's Breakfast Menu

Child Traditional English Breakfast
Fresh scrambled eggs, sausage links, English bacon, baked
beans, grilled tomato, sautéed mushrooms and breakfast
potatoes.

Child Porridge Breakfast
Old fashioned steamed oats with fresh fruit and butter
croissant.

Child Continental Breakfast
A colorful array of fresh fruit served with croissants
accompanied with assorted jams.

Child Pancake Breakfast
Two fluffy buttermilk pancakes, crisp bacon, and link
sausage with butter croissant.

Child American Breakfast
Fresh scrambled eggs, breakfast potatoes, crisp bacon, and
link sausage with butter croissant.

Children's Lunch and Dinner Menu
For ages 9 and under. All meals served with grapes &

applesauce.

Fish & Chips - $7.49 includes chips and grapes
Chicken Legs (rotisserie) - $7.49
Chicken Fingers - $7.49
Macaroni Cheese - $7.49

Side Items

Roasted Potatoes - $4.49 garlic herb roasted
Baked Potato - $4.49 topped with butter & sour cream
Corn on the Cob - $4.49
Seasoned Wedge Fries - $4.49
Fresh Garden Salad - $6.99 with choice of dressing
Fruit Cup - $4.79

Hog's Head Pub

At the rear of the Three Broomsticks tavern is the Hog's Head Pub. The whole family is welcome in the authentic pub where many enjoy Harry's favorite beverage, Butterbeer. Other drinks include pumpkin juice, lemonade, and cider. Adults can take a seat at the bar and sample the pub's selection of domestic and imported beers, specialty drinks, wine, spirits and mixed drinks including Hagrid's favorite, Fire Whisky.

Wink: *Look out for the large stuffed hog's head behind the bar which periodically snarls at guests.*

Hog's Head Pub Beverage Menu

Non-Alcoholic
Butterbeer
Frozen Butterbeer
Pumpkin Juice
Pumpkin Fizz

Lemonade
Sparkling Water
Natural Spring Water
Cider: nonalcoholic apple or pear
Iced Tea: Sweet, Unsweetened, Raspberry
Lemonade and Iced Tea Mix

Alcoholic
Guinness
Newcastle
Boddington's
Stella Artois
Yeungling
Miller Lite
Hog's Head Brew
Strongbow Cider

Spirits:
Fire Whiskey, Rum, Gin, Tequila, Vodka, Triple Sec

Cocktails:

Hog's Tea: Gin, Tequila, Vodka, Triple Sec, Sweet and Sour mix and Raspberry Tea

Hogs Head Bite: (version of British drink-Snakebite. Hogs Head Brew and Strongbow Cider

The Triple: A "secret" drink (formerly referred to as Deathly Hallows). The drink has equal amounts of Strongbow Cider, topped with Hog's Head Brew and then topped with Guinness.

Honeydukes

Honeydukes is a shop created to tempt wizards' fancy for sweet confections. Dumbledore was one of the shop's best customers, due to his partiality for sweets. At Honeydukes, muggles can enjoy all of the Hogwarts students favorite sweets including the ever popular Bertie Bott's Every-Flavour Beans, Exploding Bon Bons, chocolate cauldrons, cauldron cakes and the coveted Chocolate Frogs.

Magic surrounds these chocolate frogs which have been charmed to melt slowly in the hot Florida weather (however, the charm seems to have backfired because if chilled, they are so hard that they seem more like Hagrid's rock cakes). Enclosed in each package is an octagon shaped collectible Wizard Trading Card, favored by the magic community.

A note of warning: Some sweets at Honeydukes have magical surprises such as the popping sensations of Exploding Bon Bons and Fizzing Whisbees. Beware of some not so nice flavors in Bertie Bott's Every Flavor Beans!

Popular sweets at Honeydukes (subject to change):

Chocolate Frogs	Bar
Peppermint	Pepper Imps
Toads	Exploding Bon
Fudge Flies	Bons
Bertie Bott's	Honeydukes
Every Flavour	Salt Water Taffy
Beans	Chocolate
Clippy's Clip	Cauldron
Joint Clippings	Fizzing
Honeydukes	Whizbees
Candy Floss	Honeydukes
Sugar Quill	Hard Candy
Lollipop	Ton-Tongue
Honeydukes	Toffee
Milk Chocolate	

Some of the best treats from Honeydukes are for sale in the glass bakery case:

Menu

Apples
Caramel 7.00, Caramel with Nuts 7.00, Assorted Specialty 12.00

Chocolate Skeleton 6.00
Pumpkin Pasty 6.00

Fudge Special
Buy 4 pieces, get 2 free 19.80

Butterbeer Fudge 4.95, Assorted fudge 4.95

Chocolate Dipped Pretzel Wand 4.50

No Melt Ice Cream 7.00
Ginger Newt Cookie 6.00

Cararmels 4.95 each
3 for 12.00 or 5 for 20.00

Cakes

Pumpkin Cake $5.00
Cupcake $6
Cauldron Cake $11.00 (in a souvenir cauldron)

Crisped Rice Treat $3.50
Dipped Crisped Rice Treat $5.00

Wizard Trivia Question No. 28: What kind of sweet from Honeydukes did Ron say burnt a hole through his tongue?

"The thing about growing up with Fred and George is that you sort of start thinking anything's possible if you've got enough nerve."
Ginny Weasley
Harry Potter and the Half Blood Prince

CHAPTER 12: TOURING PLANS

The crafty wizards at Universal Orlando have created such a unique opportunity for muggles to experience the magic of the Harry Potter books, and now an overwhelming number of muggles travel from all ends of the earth to experience the magic. In the peak seasons or when a new attraction opens, the number of guests have to be limited due to muggle capacity laws. Alas, the poor muggles experience great frustration due to the crowds.

In my role as Ambassador of Muggle Relations, I have

created touring guides to assist muggles in the proper procession through the resort to create an enchanting experience. I have created guides for adults, parents with small children, day trippers and multiple day trippers.

On busy days especially during the summer, Spring Break, Thanksgiving Week and Christmas week, the parks may possibly reach maximum capacity early in the day. Unfortunately, since Universal Orlando does not take reservations, admittance is not guaranteed, even if you have a dated ticket! During very slow times, there should be no problem gaining entrance. There are two ways to be sure that you gain entrance on busy days:

1. Stay at an onsite hotel. Onsite hotel guests are not only guaranteed to gain admittance, but also get Early Park Admission, one hour before the park opens. In addition, if you stay at one of the three Premier hotels, you will also receive Universal Express which lets you into the short line on most attractions.

2. Buy an annual pass. Annual pass holders are always guaranteed admission into the theme parks. If you think purchasing an annual pass may be too expensive, a Seasonal annual pass costs only a few dollars more than a 3 or 4 day Park to Park pass, depending on the time of year of your visit. **Seasonal Passes have block out dates.** Refer to Chapter One.

A very important factor to figure into your plans are the season and weather. The "high" season is the busiest times of the year. The high season consists mainly of Summer, Christmas week, New Years, and Spring Break. The "low" season is in the Fall, Winter and Spring. Because of the popularity of the Wizarding World and the size limits of Diagon Alley, visiting during the low season is always my advice.

Geek Tip: Download the Universal Orlando app on your smart phone to have wait times and show times at your fingertips.

Wink: Want to ride Harry Potter and the Escape from Gringotts but afraid of roller coasters? I don't blame you. I'll ride a broom any day instead! Escape from Gringotts was designed to be a mild thrills ride! However, there is one drop. If you sit in the front row of the cart, the drop is less steep! The opposite is true on Hagrid's ride.

Wink: Check out all of the shops. Each shop in the Wizarding World carries its own unique merchandise. Shopping in Diagon Alley is an attraction itself.

Geek Tip: To save time and avoid lines for temporary lockers, enter the Wizarding World with no bags. All day lockers are available at the front of the park if you must bring one. I recommend using a lanyard which will fit your pass, room key, drivers license and credit card. If you must carry a bag, I recommend a flat fanny pack or small crossbody purse which are allowed on most rides.

Virtual Lines

As mentioned in Chapter 4, an attempt to reduce wait times when the parks have high attendance, Universal Orlando has instituted virtual lines on some attractions. The bad news is that if you arrive late or don't have a smart phone with the Universal Orlando app downloaded, you might not be able to ride Hagrid's ride—with a few exceptions for those with disabilities.

To be sure to ride Hagrid's Magical Creatures Motorbike Adventure on a busy day when it is sure to have a virtual line, follow these procedures mentioned in the previous chapter:

1. Download the Universal Orlando app on your smart

phone and create an account.
2. Arrive at the park on or before park opening time.
3. Before park opening time, open the Universal Orlando app.
4. Tap the Virtual Line Experience
5. Tap Virtual Line Venues
6. Tap the desired attraction
7. Now wait until the exact time when the park opens
8. Tap Reserve and the arrow on the right of Virtual Line Pass and select the number of guests, up to six—several virtual times should pop up. Tap a time as fast as you can because they go quickly. If you fail to get a time, ask the attendant at the ride. Sometimes they offer more chances for virtual line times at different times during the day such as 9am, 11am and 2:00pm.
9. You will receive a code. Screenshot this code for just in case. There have been reports of guests being unable to access their code.

*These instruction are subject to change with app updates.

Wink: *Have other members of your party try to get a virtual line time for more chances to ride!*

Wizard Trivia Question No. 29: What was the name of Harry Potter's paternal grandmother?

The One-Day Touring Plan

To take advantage of this plan, you must have a park to park ticket or annual pass. To have the best experience, I recommend touring early in the morning to avoid crowds. Arrive at the Universal's Island of Adventure entrance gate 45 minutes prior to the posted park opening time. Allow 20-30 minutes to park and go through security. If staying onsite and using free transportation, allow at least 30 minutes to arrive at the parks unless you are walking from the Hard Rock Hotel which is only a five minute walk.

Geek Tip: If you have access to Early Park Admission to either theme park, take advantage! This is the best time to take photos without crowds!

Geek Tip: To save time on a one day trip, purchase an interactive wand before arrival. Wand are available online at UniversalOrlando.com, at onsite hotels, CityWalk and the Orlando International Airport.

Start at Islands of Adventure

• Upon entry, proceed through the Port of Entry area and turn right to proceed into Seuss Landing. Turn left at Green Eggs & Ham Cafe and follow the path around to the end and turn left to enter the Lost Continent. Continue to Hogsmeade and to the line at Hagrid's Magical Creatures Motorbike Adventure.

• After riding Hagrid's ride, if the Hogwarts Express is open, ride it to the London Waterfront in Universal Studios.

• At the London Waterfront, enter Diagon Alley through Leicester Station. Prepare to be amazed at entering the world of magic!

• Proceed to Harry Potter and the Escape from Gringotts (look up if you hear the dragon grumbling, to see a fiery surprise)

• Ride Harry Potter and the Escape from Gringotts.

• Walk straight to Ollivanders for "The Wand Chooses the Wizard" ceremony and purchase an interactive wand in the shop afterwards.

• By this time you may be hungry for lunch. Proceed to the

Leaky Cauldron to enjoy British fare or try the pasties at The Hopping Pot. The London Taxi Hut at the London Waterfront has wonderful jacket potatoes which are great for lunch.

- Follow the map included with your interactive wand to cast spells in Diagon Alley, but keep your ears peeled for the music of Celestina Warbeck one of the puppet shows inspired by *The Tails of Beedle the Bard.*

- Explore Knockturn Alley and visit Borgin and Burkes. Be sure cast spells in Knockturn Alley.

- Exit Diagon Alley and say hello to the conductor at the Knight Bus before boarding the Hogwarts Express at Kings Cross Station.

- Back in Hogsmeade, ride Harry Potter and the Forbidden Journey. If you suffer from motion sickness, do the castle tour which is just walking through the queue. Feel free to spend as much time as you want going through the queue (a good time to do the Castle Tour is early morning or just before closing time).

- Spend some time casting spells in the shop windows in Hogsmeade. Visit the shops such as Honeydukes, and Owl Post (mail a postcard from owl post with the Hogsmeade postmark).

- Ride Flight of the Hippogriff.

- Dinner at the Three Broomsticks. Check the closing time in advance because the restaurant closes earlier than the park.

The Two-Day Touring Plan

To take advantage of this plan, you must have a park to

park ticket. Arrive at **Universal Islands of Adventure** 45 minutes to one hour before the posted opening time. Use the Universal Orlando app to check park hours, showtimes and wait times.

Day One

- Upon entry, proceed through the Port of Entry area and turn right to proceed into Seuss Landing. Turn right at Green Eggs & Ham Cafe and follow the path to the Lost Continent. Continue to Hogsmeade and to the line at Hagrid's Magical Creatures Motorbike Adventure (a virtual line time might be required.

- Ride the Hagrid's Magical Creatures Motorbike Adventure. Check the wait time on the app if arriving later. If the wait time is long, a light breakfast before arrival is advised. If you are unable to ride, try again today later after 2:00pm.

- Do the original Ollivanders Wand Chooses the Wizard show and purchase an interactive wand (or purchase your wand in advance in CityWalk or at your hotel).

- Ride Harry Potter and the Forbidden Journey.

- If you are ready for lunch, head to the Three Broomsticks.

- After lunch, explore, cast spells and shop in Hogsmeade.

- Ride the Hogwarts Express to the London Waterfront.

- Enter Diagon Alley through Leicester Station.

- Go directly to Harry Potter and the Escape from Gringotts and ride the attraction if the wait time is under 60 minutes. If it is longer, you may want to ride late in the afternoon.

- Exchange your currency for Gringotts bank notes and

speak to the Goblin on duty at Gringotts Money Exchange.

- Get fitted for robes at Madam Malkin's.

- Try the ice cream at Florean Fortescue's Ice Cream Parlour. If you are lucky, you can catch a show in Carkitt Market while enjoying the ice cream—either Celestina Warbeck and the Banshees or The Tales of Beedle the Bard.

- Visit Knockturn Alley and Borgin and Burkes.

- If the Islands of Adventure is open after dark, consult the Universal app for the Hogwarts Castle lights show. If the show time is within an hour, travel back to Hogsmeade by riding the Hogwarts Express. If the train wait time is more than 40 minutes, it may be quicker to walk to the other park.

- Purchase a Butterbeer or other magical beverage to enjoy while watching the light show at the castle.

Day Two

Arrive 45 minutes early at the entrance to Islands of Adventure or take advantage of Early Park Admission for onsite hotel guests.

- Head to Hogsmeade. If you were unable to ride Hagrid's Magical Creatures Motorbike Adventure on the previous day, begin your day by repeating the previous day's first step. A virtual line time may be required. Most guests try to ride at least once a day but if it is crowded, it may not be possible.

- Ride Harry Potter and the Forbidden Journey if you have not yet ridden.

- Check out the Marauders Map and other merchandise as

you exit the ride at Filch's Emporium of Confiscated Goods.

- Have breakfast or early lunch at The Three Broomsticks.

- Spend some time exploring, casting spells and sight seeing or shopping in Hogsmeade. Be sure to look up to see the Owl clock tower and shop for sweets in Honeydukes.

- Ride Flight of the Hippogriff.

- Head to Diagon Alley on the Hogwarts Express.

- Say hello to the conductor and shrunken head at the Knight bus.

- Have a wizard photo shoot at Shutterbuttons.

- Spend some time in the shops, especially Weasley's Wizard Wheezes, Madame Malkins, Quality Quidditch Supply and Magical Menagerie.

- Have dinner at the Leaky Cauldron.

- Enjoy a cauldron cake or other sweet treat from Sugarplum's. You can also try a magical beverage at The Fountain of Fair Fortune.

Three Day Touring Plan

A three day plan allows for more complete immersion into the wizarding world with more time to explore all the little nooks and crannies of these area. My advice is to always try each day to ride Hagrid's Magical Creatures Motorbike Adventure each day, since it is the most popular ride in the resort. If you are visiting during the busy season, alter this plan and always start with the previous instructions and try to obtain a virtual line time. It is always a good idea to use Early Park Admission if you are staying at an onsite hotel.

Day One

- Enter **Universal Studios**. Walk straight through Minion Land to New York and turn right at the Macy's store front. Walk straight through San Francisco until you reach the London Waterfront and enter Diagon Alley through Leicester Station.

- Have breakfast at the Leaky Cauldron.

- Visit Ollivanders, The Wand Chooses the Wizard show and purchase an interactive wand in the shop after the show.

- Go to Gringotts Money Exchange and speak to the Goblin. Exchange your currency for Gringotts Bank Notes.

- Explore Diagon Alley and cast spells.

- If you are hungry now, exit Diagon Alley and order a Jacket Potato for lunch from the London Taxi Hut.

- Explore the London Waterfront. Be sure to peruse all of the shop windows and look for Kreacher at Grimauld Place.

- Enter Diagon Alley and ride Harry Potter and the Escape from Gringotts.

- After the ride, order ice cream at Florean Fortescue's Ice Cream Parlour.

- Enter Kings Cross Station and ride the Hogwarts Express to Hogsmeade Station.

- Ride Hagrid's ride.

- If the park is open late tonight, grab a Butterbeer and watch the Nighttime Lights show on Hogwarts Castle.

Day Two

- Open the app and get a virtual ride time for Hagrid's ride if required today.

- Enter **Islands of Adventure**. Turn right at Confisco Grill, then turn left at the Green Eggs & Ham Cafe. Follow the path around and turn left to enter the Lost Continent. Enter Hogsmeade and ride Hagrid's Motorbike Adventure (or later if your virtual line is at a later time).

- Have breakfast at the Three Broomsticks.

- After breakfast, explore all of the Hogsmeade shop windows and cast spells.

- Catch a performance of the Frog Choir or TriWizard Spirit Rally.

- Order a Butterbeer from one of the red keg stands.

- Ride Flight of the Hippogriff and enjoy the spectacular view of the park.

- If you are getting hungry, the only dining option in Hogsmeade is the Three Broomsticks. Try the fish and chips, chargrilled ribs or a cottage pie for lunch.

- Shop at Dervish and Banges, Owl Post and Filch's Emporium of Confiscated Goods.

- For dessert, visit Honeydukes for a sweet treat from the bakery case.

- If you need to sit and relax, order at the Hogs Head Pub. If the weather is nice, there is outdoor seating in the back to enjoy your beverage with a view of the VelociCoaster.

- Ride Harry Potter and the Forbidden Journey.

Day Three

On day three, this is the day to catch up on anything you may have missed. If you have not yet ridden any of the rides, this should be your first priority. This day is a slower paced day for exploring and greeting some of the characters around the lands.

- Enter **Islands of Adventure**.

- Ride Hagrid's Motorbike Adventure.

- Have breakfast at the Three Broomsticks or instead try a baked treat from Honeydukes.

- Try to catch a performance on the Hogsmeade stage and take photos with the student performers after the show.

- Have a conversation with the Hogwarts Express conductor.

- Ride the Hogwarts Express from Hogsmeade Station to London.

- Have a conversation with the Knight Bus conductor and the shrunken head.

- Enter the red phone booth and dial M A G I C on the telephone.

- Enter Diagon Alley and ride Harry Potter and the Escape from Gringotts.

- Dine at the Leaky Cauldron.

- Explore Diagon Alley shops. There is always something you have not yet noticed.

- Use the door knocker at the Daily Telegraph and listen for a response.

- If you need a snack or a drink, try the Cornish Pasties at the Hopping Pot and pair that with a magical beverage such as Fishy Green Ale, Otter's Fizzy Orange or Peachtree Fizzing Tea. For something a little stronger, try one of the two exclusive brews—Dragon Scale or Wizards Brew—or Hagrid's favorite, Fire Whisky.

- With your remaining time, try to get on a ride.

- For a finale to your trip here are my suggestions: return to Hogsmeade for the Nighttime Lights on Hogwarts Castle or bide your time until closing time and try to view either Hogsmeade or Diagon Alley after all of the guests have exited.

Geek Tip: At the Hopping Pot, Fountain of Fair Fortune or the Hogs Head Pub, try this cocktail, popular with locals: Combine a shot of Fire Whiskey with Strongbow Cider.

"I can teach you how to bewitch the mind and ensnare the senses. I can tell you how to bottle fame, brew glory, and even put a stopper in death."
Severus Snape
Harry Potter and the Sorcerer's Stone

CHAPTER 13: WIZARDING WORLD'S BEST OF THE BEST

The following list was conceived by surveying guests favorites, best selling items as well as the author's personal opinion.

Wizard Trivia Question No. 30: What is the middle name of Harry and Jenny Potter's daughter, Lily?

Best Ride

10. Hagrid's Magical Creatures Motorbike Adventure

11. Harry Potter and the Escape from Gringotts

12. Harry Potter and the Forbidden Journey—this was number one on my list for many years...but due to the high number of muggles who suffer from motion sickness, its status has sadly been lowered. It is a possibility that a dark wizard cast an enchantment on this ride.

Best Themed Area

1. Diagon Alley—this spot rates number one because the absolute immersion in the wizarding world.

2. Hogsmeade—the Castle says it all.

3. The London Waterfront—the Knight Bus, Kreacher and lots of *Winks*.

Best Iconic Sight

1. Hogwarts Castle, Hogsmeade

2. Gringotts Bank, Diagon Alley

3. Weasley's Wizard Wheezes storefront, Diagon Alley

Best Ride Queue

4. Harry Potter and the Forbidden Journey—the sheer number of iconic images and props in this queue earn it the number one spot.

5. Hagrid's Magical Creatures Motorbike Adventure—there are too many Winks to count in this imaginative queue.

6. Harry Potter and the Escape from Gringotts—this queue captures the essence of the grumpy goblins.

Best Souvenir

There are too many to count, but here are a few top souvenirs…

1. Interactive wand, Ollivanders—there can be no better use of your souvenir budget than to purchase a wand to cast spells in Hogsmeade and Diagon Alley.

2. House Robe—House robes are available for each Hogwarts house with a pocket for your wand. They are made of breathable fabric.

3. Marauders Map, Filch's Emporium for Confiscated Goods—this great souvenir will allow you to keep up on the antics of several of your favorite characters in the castle.

Best Beverage

1. Hot ButterBeer or your favorite version—the warm version of Butterbeer is quintessential to the wizarding world.

2. Fire Whiskey—Hagrid's favorite adult beverage has warmed the tummy of many a muggle.

3. Pumpkin Fizz—available only at the Hogs Head and Three Broomsticks, this fizzy version of pumpkin juice is a magical drink!

Best Savory Food

1. Loaded Jacket Potato, London Taxi Hut at the London Waterfront—this street food, no matter how topped, are a delicious and satisfying meal.

2. Ploughman's Platter, Leaky Cauldron—this is a British wizards version of a charcuterie platter with cheeses, scotch eggs and more.

3. Bangers & Mash, Leaky Cauldron—these British style sausages are complimented by tasty mashed potatoes.

Best Eatery

1. Leaky Cauldron—this eatery is has the most authentic menu of what Harry would eat in his world.

2. Three Broomsticks—this restaurant has more American style options as well as Harry's favorite, Shepherd's Pie.

3. London Taxi Hut—the jacket potatoes here are fantastic!

Best Dessert

1. Strawberry peanutbutter ice cream at Florean Fortescue's Ice Cream Parlour—what can I say? This is Harry Potter's favorite flavor.

2. Freshly Baked Apple Pie at the Three Broomsticks—it is not only a deliciously spiced apple pie with raisins but at $3.99 is a great value and great for sharing. Order the vanilla or Butterbeer ice cream to go with it and you will have a flavor explosion in your taste buds.

3. Butterbeer Potted Cream—available at the Leaky Cauldron.

Best Candy Sweets

1. Chocolate Frog—this is my pick, not just for the high quality chocolate, but for the collectible wizard card included.

2. Peppermint Toads—these small peppermint flavored chocolate shapes are great for sharing and known to settle your tummy after too much Fire Whiskey!

3. Exploding Bon Bons—this magical treat invented by the Weasley brothers has an exciting spark

WIZARD TRIVIA ANSWERS

1. Harry Potter named his owl Hedwig after reading the name in the book, *A History of Magic*.

2. When asked his name by Stan Shunpike, the Knight Bus conductor, Harry gave the first name he could think of, Neville Longbottom.

3. Pavarti Patil's twin sister is Padma. She is a Ravenclaw.

4. At Weasleys Wizard Wheezes, Jenny chose a Pigmy Puff as her magical pet to take to Hogwarts Castle. He is called Harold.

5. The name of the goblin clerk who takes Harry and

Hagrid to his vault for the first time is Griphook.

6. The four houses of Ilvermorny Academy are: **Thunderbird** – the soul of the wizard, adventurers, **Horned Serpent** – the mind of the wizard, scholars, **Wampus** – the body of the wizard, warriors and **Pukwudgie** – the heart of the wizard, healers

7. The Mirror of Erised's inscription says "Erised stra ehru oyt ube cafru oyt on wohsi" which reversed and spaced properly translates to "I show not your face but your heart's desire".

8. Tom Riddle is the son of Tom Riddle Senior, a muggle, and Merope Gaunt, a descendant of Salazar Slytherin. They met in Little Harrington, England.

9. Buckbeak, the Hippogriff, was renamed Witherwings when he was left in Hagrid's care after Sirius Black's death for his protection.

10. In the book, *Harry Potter and the Order of the Phoenix*, Harry Potter took Cho Chang on a date on Valentine's Day to Puddifoot's Tea Shop, a popular spot for sweethearts in Hogsmeade.

11. Hogwarts History of Magic Professor Cuthburt Binns was a wizard but is now a ghost. He taught until a very old age, when he fell asleep in the staff room and died in slumber. Afterwards, he became a ghost who continued to teach. Students consider his class (except Hermione) as their most boring subject.

12. One gold Galleon is worth 17 silver Sickles or 493 bronze Knuts. The Galleon is thought to be worth about five pounds in U. K. currency.

13. Horned slugs are useful in potions including a potion to treat boils.

14. In the trophy case, on the Gryffindor Quidditch plaque, James Potter is the 1970 Seeker champ. R. J. King was champ in 1969 and M. G. McGonagall was champ in 1971.

15. Ginny Weasley named Ron's owl, Pigwidgeon. Ron tried to change the name, but the little owl refused to answer to any other.

16. Godric Gryffindor, one of the four founders of Hogwarts School of Witchcraft and Wizardry, was the original owner of the Sorting Hat.

17. Moaning Myrtle's full name is Myrtle Elizabeth Warren.

18. Cedric Diggory randomly picked a Swedish Short Snout dragon out of the bag for the first challenge for Challenge of Champions.

19. Weasley's Wizard Wheezes is located at 93 Diagon Alley, London, England.

20. The vampire who attends Professor Slughorn's party is Sanguini.

21. Tonks' (Nymphadora or as her father calls her, Dora) is the daughter of Andromeda Black Tonks.

Her aunts are Narcissa Malfoy and Bellatrix Lestrange. Her cousin is Draco Malfoy.

22. Essence of Dittany is known and used for its extremely effective healing properties.

23. Like the Dark Lord, Dolores Umbridge is a half blood witch, whose middle name is Jane.

24. The Sword of Gryffindor is encrusted with Rubies, the same stones which represent Gryffindor House at Hogwarts is the hourglass that counts the house points.

25. Dolores Umbridge served as Senior Undersecretary to the Minister for Magic under Minister Cornelius Fudge. She also served this role under Ministers Rufus Scrimgeour, and Pius Thicknesse.

26. Harry was with Ron and Hermione at the Three Broomsticks when he overheard Minister Fudge say that not only were Sirius and James Potter best friends, but that Lily and James had named Sirius as Harry's Godfather.

27. Hagrid brought Harry chocolate and raspberry ice cream on his first visit to Diagon Alley while he was being fitted for school robes.

28. Ron told Harry that when he was seven, Fred gave him an Acid Pop and it burnt a hole right through his tongue. Mrs. Weasley then walloped Fred with her broomstick.

29. Harry Potter's paternal grandmother was Euphemia

Potter. She was the wife of Fleamont Potter with whom she had one son, Harry's father, James.

30. Harry and Jenny Potter's daughter's full name is Lily Luna Potter. She is named for his mother and their good friend, Luna Lovegood.

SOURCES

Books:

Harry Potter and the Philosopher's Stone, J. K. Rowling, 1997
Harry Potter and the Chamber of Secrets, J. K. Rowling, 1998
Harry Potter and the Prisoner of Azkaban, J. K. Rowling, 1999
Harry Potter and the Goblet of Fire, J. K. Rowling, 2000
Harry Potter and the Order of the Phoenix, J. K. Rowling, 2003
Harry Potter and the Half Blood Prince, J. K. Rowling, 2005
Harry Potter and the Deathly Hallows, J. K. Rowling, 2007

Films:

Harry Potter and the Sorcerer's Stone, 2001
Harry Potter and the Chamber of Secrets, 2002
Harry Potter and the Prisoner of Azkaban, 2004
Harry Potter and the Goblet of Fire, 2005
Harry Potter and the Order of the Phoenix, 2007
Harry Potter and the Half-Blood Prince, 2009
Harry Potter and the Deathly Hallows I, 2010
Harry Potter and the Deathly Hallows II, 2011

Websites:

harrypotter.wikia.com
www.pottermore.com
www.imdb.com
UniversalOrlando.com
OrlandoInformer.com
www.fandom.com/universe/harry-potter

AUTHOR' NOTE

A s a born and bred "Cajun," I grew up surrounded by the folklore of the swamps of Louisiana. As a child, stories of "The Loup Garou" enchanted and filled me with fear. Another legend of displaced lovers in Henry Wadsworth Longfellow's poem, Evangeline, captivated my spirit. In Louisiana, there is a rich Native American heritage with is reflected in names of places nearby my home such as Houma, Choctaw and Coushatta. There has always been a mysticism associated with the legends of Native Americans.

As I grew into adulthood, I often traveled to the state of Florida on family vacations, visiting the white sand beaches and the emerald water of the Gulf of Mexico. I first visited Walt Disney World at a young age which started a life-long love of Orlando theme parks.

As a Harry Potter geek, I was a late bloomer. At the urging of my son, I read all seven books of the Harry Potter series by J. K. Rowling and was hooked! I watched all the movies and opened a Pottermore account. After all of this prep, I couldn't have been more excited at the prospect of visiting The Wizarding World of Harry Potter by Universal Orlando.

Many people ask me about my inspiration for writing a travel guide with a fictional character who narrates the guide. I wanted a strong female voice in my writing and I thought J. K. Rowling would appreciate a high ranking female in the Magical Congress.

My idea for writing this guide was sparked when I thought about the magical associations in Orlando in both Walt Disney World and at Universal Orlando. After all, my first book about Orlando was Universal Orlando Magic Tips. As I was thinking of this, I came up with the notion of an

American witch introducing muggles to the wizarding world at Universal Orlando (this was long before the announcement of the film, Fantastic Beasts and Where to Find Them). I decided that the original narrator should be Native American. My original thought for her name was Marietta Blackwater. I came up with the last name, Blackwater, because I remembered a visit to the Blackwater State Park near Destin, Florida.

I liked the name Marietta because it is a version of my own name and there is a character named Marietta Edgecombe in *Harry Potter and the Order of the Phoenix*. She was Cho Chang's best friend but also the student who betrayed Dumbledore's Army to Professor Umbridge. I couldn't let my American Ambassador's name have such an affiliation.

After debating on the name, I had a revelation as I read a sign on my next trip to Florida while traveling east on Interstate 10, when I passed an exit for a town called Marianna and I knew instantly that my witch's name should be Marianna Blackwater!

For my 2024 edition, I decided to introduce a new Ambassador of Muggle Relations. I love the name, Nigel, and thought that a narrator from the Ministry of Magic would be appropriate for this edition.

I like the idea of offering a different point of view than most travel guides offer. Harry Potter fandom deserved more than just the standard stating of the facts. I wanted to tell a story and encourage the readers' imagination. I hope readers notice all the details of magic on their visit and encourage their own sense of creativity when touring the theme parks. I also hope to foster generations of guests to keep reading these books and encourage their children to expand their imaginations with stories of magic.

Thank you for reading my travel guide and I hope you have many great trips to The Wizarding World of Harry Potter at Universal Orlando.

ABOUT THE AUTHOR

Mary deSilva is a muggle from Louisiana. She a graduate of the University of Louisiana. She is an author, artist, teacher, foodie and avid traveler. At the insistence of her son, she read all seven Harry Potter books back to back and watched all of the movies. She is now a self-proclaimed "Harry Potter Geek." She has published over 20 travel books.

For more information, Facebook: @MaryDesilvaAuthor

Follow on Instagram: @maryfdesilva

YouTube channel: @MaryDeSilvaCajunDIYDiva

Artwork can be found at FineArtAmerica.com and pixels.com

Blog: DestinationsDiva.blogspot.com

Printed in Great Britain
by Amazon

40729459R00098